BOOKKEEPING:

THE ESSENTIAL GUIDE FOR
BEGINNERS YOU NEED TO IMPROVE
YOUR PROFITS AND DECREASE
EXPENSES DEVELOPING INTELLIGENT
ACCOUNTING PRINCIPLES AND
EFFECTIVE HABITS FOR AN ATOMIC
BUSINESS GROWTH.

CHRIS FINANCE

TABLE OF CONTENTS

Introduction

There is no doubt that an effective bookkeeping and accounting system is the key to running a successful business. The art of bookkeeping and accounting systems is to understand the financial aspects of your business. A business will fail if it doesn't maintain good records of its transactions. A business can do well in all other aspects, but if it fails in its financial aspects, such a business will crumble.

The success of a business is determined by several factors, of which bookkeeping and accounting is a very important one. Success in business is not determined by how many sales you made or the profit you generated but by how you kept track of your transactions. The question is, how will you realize the profits generated and the sales you made if you do not keep records of your transactions?

It is only when you keep up-to-date financial records of your transactions that you can determine the performance of your business. A business is operated to generate profit, but this goal can be hindered if one fails to maintain an effective bookkeeping and accounting system.

The art of bookkeeping is an essential aspect of a business. Some small businesses failed - not because they did not make sales, or they failed to produce good products - but they failed to maintain an effective bookkeeping and accounting system.

We do not just emphasize the importance of bookkeeping and accounting because we want to force business owners to do it. The importance of bookkeeping and accounting is explained because it is vital for becoming a successful business owner and is important for both small and large businesses.

No matter how small your business is, you need to keep good track of all transactions. When you operate a business, you will certainly carry out some transactions, and these transactions should not be left unrecorded. This book was written to explain how to appropriately track those transactions.

Businesses operate well when effective bookkeeping and accounting systems are managed. To understand the art of bookkeeping, one needs to understand some basic concepts. A business should be operated to achieve success, not only to make a profit.

You must have heard of the word bookkeeping on one or two occasions. In the business world, bookkeeping is not a new thing. It has existed for so long. When we talk about bookkeeping, the first thing that comes to people's minds is that bookkeeping is the art of keeping books.

Bookkeeping is different from that; it is a broad terminology in financial accounting that entails the process of keeping good records of all financial transactions in a business.

If you want to make wise decisions in your business, then you need to practice effective bookkeeping. Bookkeeping helps you to make better decisions in your business. As a business owner, you need to make good decisions that will have a positive effect on your business. A bad decision can ruin your business and leave you with no choice than to shut down your business.

Decision making is a vital aspect of a business. You cannot make good decisions if you don't know anything about bookkeeping. Bookkeeping reveals areas where a business is lagging. With this information, you can set new goals to fix the problems in these areas.

Chapter 1.   What Is Bookkeeping

Bookkeeping, in simple terms, can be defined as the simple act of keeping stock of your business activities. When we talk about the basics associated with bookkeeping, we can align it to a small business where you can quickly write down all you have in the little shop as you record all the items that come into the shop and what goes out of the shop.

The term bookkeeping is quite easy to understand and, as the name implies, is simply comprised of a book where you keep a record of income and outgoings for business purposes. It includes every one of the transactions of the business carried out within an organization. However, so as to get a full understanding of bookkeeping, let's take a look at it from the perspective of a small business owner.

Take this scenario for example. Mrs. Adams is planning to open a small supermarket for basic home necessities in the neighborhood. She has the store filled with toiletries, soap, detergent and other much-needed home supplies and materials. However, Mrs. Adams knows she has to keep a full record of her stock and the prices they were purchased for (cost) before she finally opens the supermarket to the public. This is her first step to ensuring bookkeeping - taking inventory of the shop contents and her expenses. In her inventory, she will also include the cost of renting the store as well as the overall cost of opening the store.

Now, after she has done all of this, her shop is ready for people to start patronizing it. Her next step will, however, be opening a new book to take into account what is being bought from the store (sales). With this record, she will be able to determine her income, loss and profit as well as deciphering whether or not there are fast moving products/goods compared to others. With this, she has fully used the potential of basic bookkeeping.

This small example has defined simply what bookkeeping is for a small business within a neighborhood. However, as the business continues to grow, the basics she indulges in start becoming even more complex and more complicated bookkeeping ventures will be required, as we'll discuss later.

However, before we continue to go into detail, it is important that you have a good knowledge of some of the basic terminology used in a bookkeeping account.

Tracking the money: This involves the bank recording cash and reconciling the cash, which records the process of the cash flow from where the transaction originates and where it ends.

Earning money: This involves income, which includes all money coming into the organization.

Who wants my money: This is a record of your creditors, loan providers and tax regulators. It involves money going out vs. money coming in.

Financial Statement: This is a statement of the account that shows all of the transactions and calculations that comprise the activities of the business.

Income Statement: This statement shows all the earnings of the business in total and is explained further later in the book. It is an integral part of the financial statements.

Balance Sheet: Another integral part of the account sheets, which shows the calculation of how the business is faring.

Some abbreviations for your basic knowledge of bookkeeping, which you will come across in your study, include:

A/C- stands for Account

A/R – stands for Account Reactivated

A/P - Accounts Payable

B/S - Balance Sheet

PL - Profit and Loss

PAT- Profit after Tax

PBT- Profit before Tax

CP - a Cash Payment

EBT - Earnings before Tax

EAT - Earnings after Tax

These are a few abbreviations you have to be familiar with as you continue learning about bookkeeping from the simple process to the complex process.

Chapter 2.   The Differences Beetween Accounting And Bookkeeping

To the untrained mind, you may not find much difference between a bookkeeper and an accountant. Most people use both terms interchangeably as if they mean the same thing.

So what is the difference between accounting and bookkeeping?

Both are very different and perform different duties and functions as they have different training. To understand the difference between accounting and bookkeeping, we have to look at each of them separately.

The principle of accounting is different from that of a bookkeeper and the way to differentiate between them is through the tasks they handle. An accountant places more focus on calculating and forecasting using figures. The responsibility of the accountant includes calculating yearly profits, tax deduction, salaries deductions and other financial projections. A person is declared an accountant after the person has undergone professional training to acquire the knowledge and understand of the principles of accounting.

On the other hand, a bookkeeper is trained to make records of daily financial activities of an organization, such as recording invoices, receipts, payments made including salaries and any daily financial transactions that occur in a company. A bookkeeper does not make any calculation or projections for the company, and does not require an understanding of the principles of accounting to carry out their duties. For example, in a warehouse that deals with the mass distribution of grain, the job of the bookkeeper includes taking stock; taking a note of the number of bags in the warehouse. The bookkeeper will also be responsible for keeping a record of the number of bags that leave the warehouse, including the quantity of bags delivered to each client. The bookkeeper also takes stock of other things in the company like equipment, number of workers, working hours of the employees and so on.

The job of the bookkeeper ends at taking stock while, at this stage, the accountants come in and use the data provided by the bookkeeper to compile information about the company, which is more complex. The accountant provides the financial statement with the data obtained by the bookkeeper. So the process of bookkeeping will make no sense without the input of the accountants.

We can now understand and differentiate between bookkeeping and accounting and the principles involved in running the duties of both, as well as the kind of qualifications, training, as well as study required for both professionals. A bookkeeper can be trained in house, whereas an accountant needs recognized qualifications.

You can see that bookkeeping seems less complicated than accounting; anyone can quickly learn and apply the simple act of bookkeeping in managing their business. Although both deal with financial data, accounting will require you to go through a professional course, with in-depth knowledge of the principles of accounting. In most cases, one person can handle both tasks, as most companies use the term, bookkeeping and accountant interchangeably. It is, however, imperative that a beginner knows the difference and what each does in the process.

Chapter 3. The Importance Of Bookkeeping

Bookkeeping is an accounting concept that refers to the act of recording, verifying, retrieving, storing, and organizing the financial transactions carried out in a business or organization. Bookkeeping is sometimes called record keeping. Bookkeeping is an aspect of financial accounting that deals with recording financial transactions and events in a business or organization.

Bookkeeping can be carried out manually or with the use of bookkeeping software. The principles of financial accounting lie in keeping accurate and up-to-date records. Therefore, bookkeeping is the basis of financial accounting. It is the source of information for most of the accounting systems.

Bookkeepers are trained to use their analytical skills in recording financial transactions because most accounting information is sourced from these financial records. There are different aspects of financial accounting; these include bookkeeping, auditing, share valuation, financial forecasting, etc. Without bookkeeping, none of these aspects can function; bookkeeping is the backbone of financial accounting.

Bookkeeping provides well-detailed and accurate information from which other accounts like balance sheets, trading, profit and loss accounts, ledgers, and depreciation, among others, are prepared.

Without bookkeeping, none of these accounts can be prepared. Bookkeeping is a vital aspect of financial accounting.

Each financial transaction in a business must be recorded. There are ways in which these transactions are recorded. Bookkeeping does not only involve the recording of figures, but it also records financial transactions and events. Bookkeeping is essential for a business to thrive.

The concepts of bookkeeping and accounting are often used interchangeably, although they are separate. Bookkeeping is a vital aspect of accounting, while accounting is the general way of managing a business's finances. A person who studies bookkeeping is referred to as a bookkeeper.

A bookkeeper must understand some accounting principles and how transactions should be recorded. The process of recording and organizing transactions is called bookkeeping. Accounting is a broader concept and should not be mistaken for bookkeeping. Bookkeeping is simply an aspect of financial accounting.

Gone are the days when bookkeeping was done manually, the process of recording and organizing financial transactions has been made easier in today's world. Bookkeeping can be carried out via computer software. There are several programs used for recording and organizing transactions.

Keeping accurate and up-to-date records of all transactions is vital in bookkeeping. Bookkeeping is useless if the transactions recorded are not accurate. The most important factor in bookkeeping is accuracy. Bookkeeping is done to offer well-detailed and accurate information required to create accounting statements.

Chapter 4.   Types Of Bookkeeping

Since we now have a basic understanding of what bookkeeping is, we are going to take a dive at focusing on the different types of bookkeeping available within this chapter.

In case you don't know, there are quite a lot of bookkeeping types, which are differentiated, based on the kind of records they keep.

The Accrual Method of Bookkeeping

This type of accounting, which takes into account all the details of the company, is called the Accrual method. You take into account in your records the liabilities, assets and equity that can be analyzed into reporting the revenue, net income and expenses of the company. This kind of record is kept by bookkeeping and can be used on a monthly, quarterly and yearly basis to analyze the file kept by the bookkeeper.

The accrual method of bookkeeping is what is used to capture all of the activities of the company. The technique requires professional accountants in using the data and information provided by the bookkeeper in the analysis of the business. This type of bookkeeping is not particularly useful for small businesses that can make do with a simple form of bookkeeping.

It requires complex input of the transactions on an account sheet and calculations and interpretations in proving the information that will require explanation.

Revenues and Receivables

This type of bookkeeping method is under the Accrual method where revenues will be input in the particular way the money was earned, regardless of the period when it was received.

To understand this better, we have to look at an example in which the company provided a service that would cost 2,000 dollars on June 21st, after preparing a sales invoice. The money will be recorded on the revenues and assets account, which will increase by 2,000 dollars even though the money has not been paid to the company yet.

Expenses

With the Accrual method, the costs will reflect on the income section while accounting for the business. Expenses are one of the indices in a business that must be recorded accurately; it involves the flow of cash or funds away from the business. Every business must spend in its operations in the acquisition of business materials to carry out business activities.

Every business should have an expense account where the expense of running operations is recorded and information can be easily retrieved for deductions and calculations. As we go further into this book, you will realize that there are some calculations that we need in order to make up the total expenses for a set period of time in order to derive an analysis of the business.

Regarding expenses, we can determine the health of the business and whether or not it is wise to increase the expenses or decrease expenses depending on the situation that will fit the market at the time. The expenses of the business need to be monitored carefully to ensure that the business does not go in the wrong direction. In a simple analysis, especially for small scale businesses, always watch that the expenses are not more than what is coming into the system to remain in business. It is only at the initial period of starting the business that the expenses can be higher than income and that will be acceptable.

By keeping a record of the expenses, you can quickly check if the figure is higher than the amount that the company is making. Then you can analyze what you are spending on money on and how much money and look for ways to reduce expenses and increase profit.

For example, if you are the owner of an ice cream truck, you have your expense list, which includes the raw materials for the ice cream, transportation, maintenance of the vehicle, payment at the car wash, running costs of the vehicle and so on. At the end of the quarter, you notice that your expenses are a little higher than the amount you are gaining for the business.

What do you do at this instance?

The obvious answer is to check for ways to reduce expenses and/or increase profit. You'll always be on the lookout for ways to reduce expenses and therefore increase profit. Remember we are trying to maximize profit.

From the apparent list of your expenses, you can try to reduce the costs by cutting down on fuel consumption of the van. You can decide to spend time at a particular location you know you have high patronage to maximize profit and reduce expenditure. Pick locations with high patronage and spend time there rather than driving around town, thus saving on fuel costs and wear and tear.

Also, you can reduce the expenses on the car wash and do the washing yourself. With eliminating expenses in those two areas, you can analyze how helpful these changes would be to your next financial statement.

There is the recurrent expenditure of a business that occurs regularly and recording such expenses will enable the company to make plans to accommodate such costs on time. Some examples of these recurring expenditures include salaries, transportation, utilities, working materials, and so on. Since you know these are needed for the operation, then plans can be made beforehand to make money available when due.

So keeping a record of your expenses is essential because these records will be used in planning for the next financial period of the business. This is just like preparing a budget to run the business, where these recurrent costs for the operation will be known in advance and can be used to anticipate what needs to be available in the future.

Recording expenses will help you to manage your spending when you become cautious about what you spend money on, especially when you find out that some of these expenses are not relevant to the growth of the business.

The importance of keeping an expense list can be summarized in the following points:

• For proper record keeping and tracking the expenses of the business.

• In analyzing the market for profit and loss.

• In the production and determination of financial report.

• To keep track of recurrent expenditures and other forms of cost of operation.

• To keep track of the finances of the business.

Differentiating between the Accrual Method and the Cash Method

There are some noticeable differences between the Accrual method and cash method, which are listed below:

• Unlike the cash method, money owned for services rendered is recorded as an asset.

• In the Accrual method, the bookkeeper records immediately when a service fee is agreed upon while with the cash method, it is only recorded when cash exchanges hands. A good example is with a small business that makes use of the cash method. The owner of the ice cream shop will make a record when the customer has paid for the ice cream bought. In big corporations, when the deal is put on paper, it is recorded while each party makes a plan on how long it takes to finally complete payment and the length of the contract or operation. But it is already recorded in the books as the deal is struck.

• With the Accrual method, bills, loan payments and any other expenses are regarded as a liability, which is not the same as cash.

• The Accrual method records net income using revenue earned and bills, while the cash method uses just cash receipts and cash spent.

• While the Accrual method provides in details the assets, liabilities and equity, the cash method does not provide such detailed information.

From the point listed above, it is obvious that the Accrual method is most preferred since it aligns with preferred accounting principles, unlike the cash method.

Single and Double Entry Bookkeeping System

The single entry bookkeeping and the double-entry bookkeeping are the two major kinds of bookkeeping commonly used in the world today. We are going to discuss in detail the two significant types of bookkeeping including the differences, advantages and the disadvantages of the systems.

Single Entry Bookkeeping System

The history of single entry bookkeeping is sketchy because it has been around for a very long time and scientists can trace its origin as far back as 200 BC. Traders in history had adopted this method of accounting because of its ease in keeping records of simple sales.

The single entry bookkeeping system is suited for small scale businesses that want to keep things simple by recording everything with just a single account. Records and reports of cash spent, receipts of cash, purchase made and sales are reported in this single account system.

In this type of bookkeeping system, just one account will be affected as the bookkeeper records all daily, monthly and yearly cash transactions. This kind of system proves difficult for an accountant to analyze the records of such accounts because it is only a single accounting of all transactions made.

The single entry system is not as complex as the double entry system and does not require the expertise of an accountant. Anyone with little or no experience in accounting whatsoever can operate the single entry system where you are only required to fill out all the transactions in a single manner.

The single entry method is most suitable for small businesses, where only completed transactions are recorded. What we mean by this is that only effected transactions are recorded. For example, a cash transaction will be recorded in the cash account when the money and goods or products have exchanged hands and the business is complete. Assets and liabilities are not taken into account with the single entry method, unlike we do in double entry accounting.

In the case of the business getting a loan, the single entry bookkeeping will record it as cash coming in. However, it becomes difficult to register the interest from the loan. So much information cannot be acquired from single entry bookkeeping. It is a difficult task when an accountant decides to transfer data in a single entry book to a double entry book.

Advantages of Single Entry Bookkeeping

Although single entry bookkeeping does not give out more detailed information than the double-entry bookkeeping, it has its positive side.

Here is a list of some of the advantages of using single entry bookkeeping:

• It is easy to operate and anyone without knowledge of accounting can operate it. This makes it suitable for businesses that cannot afford the services of professional accountants.

• It is easy to understand and interpret by anyone looking at the business books.

• There is no need for complicated accounting software to operate the single entry bookkeeping method. All transactions can be done manually by inputting figures in the correct column.

Disadvantages of Single Entry Bookkeeping

The single entry bookkeeping may be simple, but it has so many disadvantages when being compared with the double entry system. The disadvantages are listed below:

• You cannot use this method of accounting for public companies that have to publish a statement of account. The information will be inadequate and one cannot access all the financial transactions of the company.

• You do not have records of assets and liabilities of the company, which make the book inadequate for proper accounting.

- With a single entry system, it is difficult to check for errors, unlike the double entry system, which has various tools you can use to check for errors.

- The single entry system does not support accrual accounting, which makes it impossible to analyze other transactions, such as supplies, payment of debts and so on.

- One cannot obtain an audited financial report from this kind of accounting.

- You cannot use it to seek a loan or other financial support.

- It is easy to carry out fraud with the single entry system as one can easily alter figures to tally with the total.

The choice of which of the methods of bookkeeping to use lies solely on the business owners as they have their specific advantages and disadvantages.

Double Entry Bookkeeping System

This kind of system is used both by accountants and bookkeepers with complete and well-organized details of transactions in the company. The double entry bookkeeping method is used by big companies and organizations to record their complex transactions.

You can use this account to attract investors or apply for a loan as it gives a potential lender a clue as to the performance of the company. It is easier for an accountant to make use of this system to analyze the prospects of the company.

Before advancing further, one must admit that without bookkeeping, there will be no accounting. Bookkeeping is the first step to accounting, which involves the recording of all information gathered to give a bigger picture of the company.

Now, let's shed light on the complete details of the double entry bookkeeping system so that you have a better understanding.

The double entry bookkeeping system uses an accounting principle in its operations, taking into account the liabilities of the company with the capital as assets of the company. This system is based on the two fold principles, which makes us understand that as long as there is something taken which is regarded as debt, we are getting something back, which is regarded as credit. In business, it is expected that when you obtain capital, you intend to use that capital to gain some resources for the set period - one of the principles of double entry bookkeeping.

An accountant must be able to identify which one of the elements is affected in any business transaction and to record these transactions appropriately.

The double entry method is not perfect in all areas as one may prefer to use the single entry method in some instances. There is never a perfect system and thus we have systems that have been modified from time to time to meet up with our demand for a system that will meet our individual requirements.

Advantages of Double Entry Systems

• There is a deep understanding of the financial transactions of the company that is represented effectively.

• With this system, you can keep a record of all transactions that exist in the company for it to make room for all elements.

• There are more accurate records using this method.

• You can easily analyze different periods within a transaction with this method when you want to compare and analyze different periods of time.

• The profit and loss of the company can be determined fast and easily using this system.

• You can get every transaction detailed easily with this kind of method.

Disadvantages of Double Entry Method

• The double entry method is not easy to assimilate, especially as a beginner. It is very complex to use; it takes time to understand and get used to working with.

• It is expensive to use this method in organizations.

• It is time-consuming in detailing all financial transactions in the organization.

Bookkeeping Excel vs. Bookkeeping Software

You can use bookkeeping Excel sheets for manual output, which is easier with single entry bookkeeping. There is software available that can be used to make accounting more comfortable and faster, especially when using the double entry bookkeeping.

The manual form of bookkeeping has been used for a very long time and you can make use of the Excel sheets to input your data when you use manual bookkeeping. The manual form of entering in bookkeeping can be tedious when operating within a big organization, so it is best suited for small business.

Excel sheets are available on all computers and in most cases come pre-installed, not forgetting that they are also simple to use. The Excel sheets come with prearranged sheets that you can easily input data. The sheets makes it easy to work with, such as recording data and numbers in bookkeeping. You can easily make calculations, draw tables and charts, such as bar charts and pie charts on the Excel sheets.

This makes it easy to present data in ways that can easily be analyzed. Accountants use Excel sheets to make calculations, especially with pre-installed formulas for calculating statistical parameters. You can quickly learn Excel and start using it for your business in simple deductions, making it easy to view a pictorial presentation that will help simplify data so you can easily visualize and understand it.

The installation of Excel sheets comes free with Microsoft Office, containing all that you need to prepare financial reports and other accounting reports. You can also use the Excel sheets for both single entry and double entry bookkeeping in the production of salary structure.

In preparing the salaries for the company, the Excel sheets help by putting the names and figures in good order. Also, you can get accurate calculations in this situation. You can use the Excel sheet in your bookkeeping without using any other software.

Bookkeeping software is becoming popular for both small scale businesses and large enterprises. Software makes it easy to carry out accounting duties with such accuracy and few to minimal errors.

With the software, you can work out complex calculations, analysis and other accounting functions, even if it is being operated by someone with no experience in accounting. One such useful software is called SAGE, which is easy to use and to obtain data for financial transactions. The SAGE software is an interactive program, user-friendly and easy to use as you input your data to get various accounting reports.

This software is used in the preparation of financial statements, especially with big corporations. Such a task cannot be performed on the Excel sheets because they need more complex calculations and deductions. The software can be adjusted to the needs of the business for easy input of data, as well as computation.

A small business might not need to waste money on such software, as the Excel sheets can do the work adequately. However, big corporations with huge accounting details will require a more complex kind of bookkeeping and accounting software.

Chapter 5.   Function Of An
Accounting Officer

It takes some of us longer to acknowledge we need help than it does others.

I interviewed my first accountant about two years after I started selling online. I was making about $1,500 a month selling on eBay at that time and I was starting to get it all together. I had a business checking account, a business credit card, and had just upgraded all of my computer equipment.

Things were looking good, and I decided having an accountant on my side could be the ace-in-the-hole I needed to be more successful.

Ok. I made my appointment. Gathered up all my receipts and printed out my reports from QuickBooks. In effect, I was ready to do battle.

I walked in, placed my bundles on the desk, and sat down opposite the accountant. I was promised a free hour's consultation, and I made sure to get in as many questions as I could. I suppose I wanted to get my money's worth – even if it was a free appointment.

When I walked out of that office I was psyched up and sure he was the guy. And, yet – I didn't add an accountant to my team for another five years. Why? Because I couldn't justify the $65.00 an hour fee several times a year.

It doesn't make any sense now. But sixty-five bucks is sixty-five bucks, and thirteen years ago, that was a lot of money.

Let me tell you what I've learned over the last ten years that justifies every penny I pay my accountant.

Perhaps the biggest reason is peace-of-mind. I'm a seat-of-the-pants type of guy, which means I normally just jump into things and do them the best I can. While that sometimes works selling on eBay or writing books, it doesn't always work the best when you're trying to manage your finances.

I still do my day-to-day accounting and my taxes myself, but I'm smart enough now to have someone peek over my shoulder now and then to make sure I'm on the right track. Sometimes I make stupid mistakes, overlook important details, or just can't see obvious mistakes. An extra set of eyes on my paperwork can point out these hidden boners (sorry for that word, but it is appropriate here).

Fortunately most of my mistakes have been small ones that are easily fixable. But, the peace-of-mind thing is still an important factor that keeps me paying my accountant's bill.

It's an extra eye on my paperwork pointing out that I spent too much on inventory last quarter, or I probably don't need to buy a new laptop every year, or have the fanciest iPhone each time they come out. Sometimes you don't see (or don't want to see) your own crazy spending habits.

Let's talk about you for a minute.

What can working with an accountant do for your business? Obviously, there's that peace-of-mind thing. They can also –

1) Help you determine how much you should pay for your quarterly tax payments.

2) Find extra deductions and credits to reduce your taxes and help you receive larger refunds.

3) Help you understand the breakeven point for your business so that you know how many sales you need to make just to cover your bills.

4) By challenging your spending habits, they can help you increase profits and make better purchasing decisions.

5) If your business is seasonal, depending more upon Christmas or summertime sales, an accountant can help you smooth out cash flow fluctuations so you can keep your business running smoothly year around.

6) Set up a retirement plan that allows you to maximize current earnings while saving more money for retirement.

7) A good accountant can help you plan for growth, or to reach other stretch goals you may have for your business.

With all of that said, how do you find a good accountant that you can work with?

Most accountants offer a free consultation. This is a chance for you to meet with them and kick the tires a little. Normally the accountant will tell you a little bit about how they like to do business and what they can do for you, and then they will throw the ball into your court and let you ask some questions.

My suggestion is to make up a list of questions before your appointment.

Ask questions about costs. Ask about how often you need to consult with them? Ask what the accountant expects from you? What papers do they need you to supply? If you're looking for help incorporating your business or setting up a retirement plan, nail down the costs. If you're looking for tips to help grow your business, make sure they have experience dealing with businesses similar to your own. Get references, and be sure to check them out.

Most importantly, don't rush into any arrangement. Interview at least two or three accountants until you find someone you feel comfortable working with.

One final note: Depending upon the accountant you chose to work with you may be asked to provide an "accountant's copy" of your records each time you come in. This makes it easier for your accountant to keep tabs on your business, and check for errors in your record keeping.

If your accountant requires an "accountant's copy" to work with you're going to need to switch to QuickBooks. GoDaddy Bookkeeping does not offer this feature.

Chapter 6. What Is An Asset

It's easy enough to understand that assets are things that have value that your company owns. But you can't just total up everything you own, then place the amount in one huge asset account. Even your company's cash reserves will have to separate into different accounts – main checking account (cash) and petty cash, with retained earnings placed in a revenue account. The reason for this specificity is to allow for more control over your company's finances. For example, you will pay all your monthly bills and routine expenses out of your cash account, but you should also fund a petty cash account, so employees have access to funds for unexpected per diem accounts and unplanned purchases. The following is a list of some of the types of accounts commonly listed under Assets:

● Cash: There may be serval cash accounts or only one, depending on the structure of your company. If you have more than one account into which you make deposits or withdraw money for purchase, each of them should be identified:

○ Petty cash

○ Business Checking

○ Business Savings

● Accounts receivable. Total amount of all unpaid invoices sent to customers for goods and services sold. This account is separate from cash because you have not received the money yet.

- Inventory. The total value of all items your company currently possesses, and that you intend to sell.

- Equipment. The total value of all business equipment that you have purchased and own outright.

- Buildings. The total value of any buildings your company owns.

- Land. The total value of all undeveloped land your company owns.

- Investments. The total value of all securities investments your company owns.

- Prepaid expenses. If your company prepays expenses such as rent or insurance, you may create an account to keep track of the value:

o Prepaid rent

o Prepaid insurance

- Supplies. This may be included as part of the equipment account, or you may create a separate account, depending on the nature and complexity of your business.

Chapter 7.   What Is A Current Assets

Current assets are going to be any that the company owns that have a lifespan that is a year or less. This means that the asset has to be easily changed over to cash if the company needs to. Such assets will include inventory, accounts receivable, and cash or cash equivalents.

Cash, which is the most fundamental and most commonly thought about the current asset, can also include checks and bank accounts that are not restricted. Cash equivalents are going to be assets that are very safe, but which can also be turned into cash quickly if the company needs. The U.S. Treasury is a good example of this. And then there are the accounts receivables, which are going to show the reader any of the obligations that customers and others owe to the company over the short-term. These sometimes happen if a company allows the customer to use credit to purchase the product or service.

Inventory is an important current asset as well. Inventory can include things like the raw materials to make a product, the products that are still in the process of being created, and the finished goods. Each company is going to be different, and the exact way that the inventory account looks is going to be different. For a manufacturing firm, there may be a lot of raw materials, but a retained firm wouldn't have any raw materials.

Chapter 8.   What Is A Non-Current Assets Liabilities

Long-Term Assets

Besides just the current assets there are some long-term assets. These assets are usually assets that you hold for periods that are more than one year. These also represent the future growth of the business.

Some of these long-term assets can include but are not limited to:

- Land
- Vehicles
- Computers
- Machinery
- Equipment
- Securities
- Stocks
- Bonds

Businesses use these long-term assets to produce revenue. The longer the asset the better. It will cut costs and make the business produce more income. This will also make your business more valuable. In return it will increase stock prices. However, you do need to be careful. It is possible to have too many long-term assets.

If you have too many then the company or business may not have enough capital and could have trouble keeping up with expenses and liabilities. However, on another note, having too few long-term assets could also harm the company. This could make it vulnerable to changes and difficult to fight against the competitors.

Fixed Assets

With fixed assets the main purpose is to create revenue. These types of assets are not to be sold. Even though fixed assets cannot be turned into cash they do enhance the value of your company.

Due to the GAAP a fixed asset must be recorded on a balance sheet at a cost value and not market value. This is considered a historical cost principle. There are several reasons why they are treated as a historical cost principle.

Cost can be easily verified in an audit. This is done by checking a receipt. Whereas, market value is highly subjective.

When a company starts it is assumed that they are not going to be selling off assets and shutting down. As long as the business intends to stay in business the market value of a fixed asset is irrelevant. This is because the function of the asset is to produce revenue and not to be sold.

According to the GAAP it is required for a company to recognize revenue and expenses in a financial period when they are earned or incurred.

The initial cost of an asset was recorded on the balance sheet when it was purchased. Therefore, the amount of depreciation must be listed as an expense over the span of life used for that asset.

Land is one of the most common and expensive fixed assets. It will include everything on ground (for example grass, fences, and trees), over the ground (for example air, space), and under the ground (such as minerals). It is supposed to have the longest lifespan or even indefinite. This is because the only thing that may shorten the lifespan of land is a natural disaster. This is a valuable asset as it usually is not used up, destroyed, or stolen. On the balance sheet it will reflect the cost of the land. With that it will also include incidental cost such as surveys, insurance, legal fees, and property taxes.

Buildings, much like land, are expensive and a valuable fixed asset. They indirectly produce revenue. The cost of acquiring buildings usually includes insurance, closing costs, taxes, and the purchase price. They do not last forever. Therefore, they have a finite lifespan.

For all business your equipment is essential. Much like buildings they indirectly produce revenue. The cost of equipment generally includes the purchase price, sales tax, and delivery fees.

While looking at the long-term assets you need to remember that any asset that is purchased and lasts more than one year is a capital expenditure. These expenditures are recorded on the balance sheet. Usually they include large purchases that bring a lot of value to your company or business. These will not be listed in expenses because they will not be used up in the current accounting period.

So we talked about the bigger assets but what about the smaller ones such as a coffee maker, trashcan, or a light bulb? These are considered revenue expenditures. These will last several accounting periods. Even though $500 is a common limit for the maximum cost of this type of expenditure it can vary based on the company or business. These assets are not recorded in the balance sheet. They are usually listed as an expense to make it easy to record them.

Depreciation

With long-term assets you will have many assets that will depreciate over time. Land is the one thing that is the exception to depreciation. Mainly because land does not depreciate. Depreciation is for those assets that are good for only a given number of years and will eventually need to be replaced. Therefore, we need to figure out how much it will depreciate over time.

Depreciation will assign a cost of a long-term asset to an expense account in the periods when the asset generates revenue. So when you think about it, depreciation basically offsets the revenue of an accounting period with the costs of the product or service consumed to generate the revenue.

The depreciation expense does not come to decrease value. Instead it is a result from allocating cost of a period of time. Once you start using the asset that is to be depreciated it is generally done quarterly or annually. The depreciation ends when the company or businesses disposes of the asset or determines that its lifespan is over.

There are several ways to record depreciation. The GAAP rule only requires the method used is rational and systematic through the asset's lifespan. Let's look at some of the ways to figure and record depreciation.

Straight-line method—this is the most common for financial reporting. It will maximize net income more than any other method. It is also the easiest to understand and follow the calculations. This method attributes an equal amount of expense to each period of lifespan for the assets. Before we can understand the calculations we first need to find out what salvage value is. When a business uses the lifespan of the asset and is ready to sale it you need to ask yourself how much you expect to earn from selling the asset. This is the salvage value. So let's look at the equation for the straight-line method:

Depreciation = (Cost – Salvage Value) / Lifespan

To explain this better let's look at each aspect of the equation. First you will take the cost of the asset and subtract the salvage value. The cost will be the original cost when you purchased the asset. Then you will take this total and divide it by the lifespan. The lifespan is the number of years that the business sees the asset as useful. This gives you the depreciation cost.

For example, you have a flow jet for your business. The estimated lifespan is five years. You originally purchased it for $20,000 and the estimated salvage value would be $5,000. Let's put this in the equation. $20,000 - $5,000 = $15,000 / 5 = $3,000. Therefore, the depreciation will be $3,000. Many times, you can think of the lifespan as a percentage. The rate is 1. So the lifespan for the flow jet will be 1/5 or 20%.

With a depreciation schedule we see the book value. It is important to know the book value of an asset. To find this you will take the original asset cost and minus the accumulated depreciation.

Book Value = Cost – Accumulated Depreciation

Market value and book value are not the same. Book value represents the value of the asset according to the business books. Each year the book value has to be updated. This is because the accumulated depreciation will change each year and the company or business needs to know when the lifespan will be up. However, the book value should never go below the salvage value of the asset. This is a conservation principle. Keep in mind that when the depreciation is finished you will see the salvage value and the book value will be equal.

Declining-balance method—with this method the depreciation assigned for each year of usage is different. Suppose that you feel that your asset is more productive and creates more revenue early in its life. This method is an accelerated method. You will see more depreciation expense allocated early in the asset's life than it would be in the later years.

For the declining-balance method we can calculate the depreciation expense with the following formula:

Depreciation Expense = Rate * Current Book Value

Since the book value decreases each period so does the depreciation expense. This is why it is called declining-balance method.

With all the methods you need to keep in mind that the book value will never go below its salvage value and it will be equal when it is at the end of its lifespan.

Sum of the Years' Digits (SOYD) method—is another accelerated method for depreciation. With this method the amount of depreciation is assigned to each year of life based on an inverted scale of the sum of the years of its lifespan.

Units of Production method—is different than the other methods. It is based on depreciation from a measurement of the asset's output instead of its lifespan. With this method it allows for more depreciation when the asset is used more. The method is more used for assets such as vehicles and machinery. For calculating this method you would use the following formula. It is similar to the formula for the straight-line method.

Depreciation Rate per Unit = (Cost – Salvage Value) / Estimated Units of Output

Keep in mind that natural resources are depreciated differently than other assets. This is because once their lifespan is up or they are used up then they can only be replaced through natural processes. To figure this you will need to first find the cost per unit.

Cost Per Unit = Depletable Cost / Estimated Total Number of Units

Once you have the cost per unit then you can calculate the depletion expense.

Depletion Expense = Cost Per Unit * Yearly Number of Units Extracted

Modified Accelerated Cost of Recovery System (MACRS) method— must be used for a business's income tax returns. Businesses are allowed to use one method for their income tax returns and another method for their financial statements. With this method the Internal Revenue Service (IRS) will specify depreciation rates and time periods for particular categories of fixed assets, for example, furniture and computer equipment. Using this method will lower net income which will lower the taxes owed to the IRS.

Chapter 9.   Current Liabilities

Liabilities are different from expenses. Think of expenses as the monthly or daily costs associated with running your business. Liabilities represent a fixed amount of money that you owe to outside third parties. Generally, you assume liabilities as part of the overall investment for starting and/or growing your business. The following are some examples of the type of Liability accounts many businesses will record in their ledgers:

• Accounts payable. All outstanding financial obligations that the company has not yet paid.

• Sales tax payable. Especially if you sell goods and services online, your company may be required to keep track of the sales tax you owe and pay the IRS annually or quarterly. This account will help you record these transactions.

• Salaries payable. Prior to distributing payroll checks to your employees, the hours they work will accumulate total amounts payable in this account.

• Retirement contributions payable. If your company provides employees with retirement accounts with matching contributions, you can record transactions here.

• Mortgage payable. If you have bought a building for your business and you still owe money on the mortgage, you should record all associated transactions here.

- Taxes payable. Your business may be responsible for a variety of tax obligations, and separate accounts can be set up for each of them:

  ○ Federal unemployment tax payable.

  ○ Federal income tax payable.

  ○ State unemployment tax payable.

  ○ State income tax payable.

  ○ Social security tax payable.

- Interest payable. If you have taken out any business loans, you can record amortized interest payable here.

Chapter 10.   Non Current Liabilities

Any time a company has obligations that carry a set value you have a known liability. The known liabilities may fall into other categories such as:

Accounts payable

Sales tax payable

Unearned revenue

Short-term notes payable

Payroll liabilities

Accrued liabilities

If you remember, any goods or services purchased on credit are considered accounts payable. However, when you make a sale it may incur yet another type of known liability. This would be sales tax payable. This account will be used for tracking and recording sales tax that needs to be paid to the state and local governments.

Also remember when a company receives money in advance it would be considered as unearned revenue. These unearned incomes can be considered as a known liability.

Another form of known liability is a short-term note payable. This is a debt that will be paid on a promissory note within one year.

An important known liability for a business is the payroll liability. The best way to think about these liabilities is the amount paid to employees and is a set amount paid on a predetermined date. This type of liability has three categories.

Employee compensation

Payroll withholdings

Payroll taxes

For this we can look at your regular paycheck. You perform 40 hours a week for two weeks at $9 per hour. This earns you $720. This would be considered your employee compensation. From that $750 there are withholdings that are deducted to fulfill tax requirements. These payroll withholdings are social security, Medicare, and federal and state income taxes. However, social security and Medicare taxes support benefits such as retirees, disabled individuals, and other types of medical programs. Instead of employees needing to pay their federal and state taxes directly to the government, your business is required to deduct this and report it for the employee. The last one is the payroll taxes. There are the withholdings from the employees that need to be paid to the government.

For an idea of how this is paid see the example:

DATE	ACCOUNT	DEBIT	CREDIT
July 31	Salary wage expense	$1,330	
	Social security tax payable		$200
	Medicare tax payable		$30
	Federal income tax payable		$1,100

There are times where an employee may request to have additional withholdings deducted from their wages. The most common are:

Insurance premium payments

Pension or retirement plan

Chapter 11.   Balance Sheets

A balance sheet is going to show the assets of the company, the liabilities of the company, and the net worth, or the owner's equity. The balance sheet will work along with the other financial documents that we have talked about in order to show a complete picture of the financial state of that company. If you hold onto stocks of that company, it is a good idea to understand more about the balance sheet, such as how it is structured, the best ways to look over and understand the sheet, and even tips for reading through the balance sheet.

How Can I Use This Financial Document?

The balance sheet is going to be split up into two parts. These two parts are going to be based on an equation, and they must either end up equaling each other or coming out so that they are balanced, or something is wrong with your numbers. The formula that is needed to work with the balance sheet will include:

Assets = Liabilities + Shareholder's Equity

What all this means is that all the assets, or the money used to operate the company, need to be balanced out by the financial obligations of the company, along with any of the equity investment that comes back to that company, and then they will be known as that company's retained earnings.

The assets are important because they are what the company will use in order to operate the business. The equity and the liabilities are going to be what will support those assets. The owner's equity, which can be known as the shareholder's equity, if the company is publicly traded, will include any of the money that the shareholders invested in that company. It can also include any retained earnings as well. This is important because it is going to represent the funding sources for that particular business.

One way that the balance sheet is different than the income statement we talked about before is that the balance sheet we talked about earlier is more of a snapshot that showcases the financial position of that company right then and there. If the accountant does this financial document on May 21, 2018, then the balance sheet will show where the company is on that date. It won't cover February 21 to May 21. It just shows May 21.

The Balance Sheet For The Securities And Exchange Commission

Just like the bank wants you to put together a balance sheet to take a look at whether they think you can do well with any credit they offer, the government is going to require that any company that is traded publicly will put together a balance sheet, usually each quarter, to show to their shareholders.

This balance sheet can be important because it will allow all potential and current investors to see a good snapshot of the finances of that company. In addition to some other things, the balance sheet is going to show you all the value of the stuff that the company owns, right down to the office supplies that the employees use, the amount of debt that the company is taking care of right now, and how much inventory is in the warehouse. It can even tell the investors about how much money the business will have available to work with through the short-term.

This balance statement is going to be one of the first financial statements that you should analyze when you want to see the value of the company. Before you can learn how to analyze this balance sheet, it is important to know how it is structured.

Before we get into this too much though, you need to understand that the limited partnership, limited liability Company, and the corporation balance sheets are going to be a lot different from the regular household balance sheet. This is mainly because these companies have a lot of complex items in their accounting records to keep the company going. This is why many of these companies rely on an accountant to help them get it done.

Businesses are often faced with many difficult questions that others may not know the answers to, such as how to depreciate out the costs for some of their business expenses, how to record the lease obligations, how to account for the expenses of construction at the power plan, and so much more.

No matter how overwhelming it can seem in the beginning to figure out all the different parts of the balance sheet, it is actually pretty simple once you have looked at a few. The best way to get through the balance sheet is to remember that the purpose of this financial statement is to answer three basic questions for anyone who is looking at that sheet. These three main questions that the balance sheet should answer include:

What does the company have? These will be the assets of the company.

What does the company owe on? These will be the liabilities of the company.

What is left over for the owners of that business if they were to pay off all their debts? This one is going to be the shareholder equity or the book value.

These are pretty advanced terms and fancy words, but they are there to help give the investor a good idea of where the business is at that time. If you can remember the objective of the balance sheet, all those fancy words and accounting complexities won't seem as overwhelming when you take a look over it later.

One thing to remember is that unlike some of the other financial statements, the balance sheet is not going to cover a range of dates. The information that is present in the balance sheet is going to be good as of the date that is on the balance sheet, but it won't be able to tell you any date ranges in the process. If you are looking to deal with this issue when calculating many of the accounting ratios, then the best way to do this is to work with the averagely weighted figures of the balance sheet.

An example of this is if you would like to figure out what the average value of inventory was for that year for the company. You would be able to do this by taking the value of the inventory at the previous yearend, add it to the inventory's value at the end of this year, and then divide them by two.

This is a quick trick that will help you to avoid any distortions by ending period figures that may or may not be able to accurately reflect what occurred throughout that year. For example, if the manufacturing business was able to pay off all the debt it had in the year and this showed that there was $0 in liabilities on this balance sheet, but then there was a line there to show the interest expense on your income statement, this could be confusing.

By taking the time to weigh the average debt outstanding from the balance sheet over that same period, you may be able to get a better idea of what the business has going on here and why they listed some interest costs on the income statement but not on the balance sheet.

Chapter 12.   Capitals

Final accounts are prepared at the end of the year and they consist of the income statement, balance sheet, cash flow statement, and the statement of retained earnings. All the accounts, which appear in the trial balance, are taken to either the income statement or the balance sheet. In order to decide which item goes where, the following principle of accounting is applied. All revenue expenditures along with receipts are taken to the income statement while all capital expenditure and capital receipts are entered in the balance sheet. It is, therefore, essential to realize the importance of distinction between capital and revenue items because any error in these items can lead to falsification of final accounts.

A capital expenditure is one that increases the value at which a fixed or a capital asset may properly be carried on in the books. All expenditure that results in the acquisition of any permanent assets that are intended to be continually used in the business purpose of earning revenue I'd deem to be capital expenditure. The term capital expenditure is usually used for signifying an expenditure, which increases the quantity of fixed assets, quality of fixed assets, or results in the replacement of fixed assets.

An amount that is spent by the business for earning or providing revenue is referred to as revenue expenditure. Revenue expenditure is one that constitutes a proper deduction from income revenue. It is an expense. In other words, all establishments and other expenses incurred in the conduct and administration of the business are deemed to be revenue expenditures. All expenses incurred by the way of repairs, replacement of existing assets, which not only add to their earning capacity but simply serve to maintain the original equipment in an efficient working condition are charged as revenue expenditures. Examples of revenue expenses include any expenditure incurred during the normal course of business. For instance, expenses of Administration, expenses incurred in manufacturing and selling products, expenses related to salaries, rent and repair of facets and so on. All those expenses which are incurred for maintaining the business like the replacement of any existing permanent assets, costs of stores consumed for manufacturing and so on are also deemed to be revenue expenditures.

Deferred revenue expenditure is the term that's used for describing any expenditure of a revenue nature with its benefits spread over a couple of years. Some common examples of deferred revenue income include preliminary expenses, brokerage payable on issue of shares, expenses incurred in shifting a business, or even any exceptional repairs. All these might look like expenses but when it comes to accounting, they aren't treated as regular expenses. Given the massive amounts involved, these expenses cannot be written off in a single financial year. If such expenses are written off from a single year's profits, then there might be no profits left. To prevent this and to maintain a profitable venture, deferred revenue expenses are written off from the income statement on a yearly basis. The unwritten portion of the deferred revenue expenditure will be reflected on the assets side of the balance sheet.

All capital receipts are reflected in the balance sheet and the revenue receipts in the income statements. Capital receipts include the proceeds from the sale of fixed assets, issue of any shares or debentures, and money received in the form of loans. Any funds obtained in the due course of business are known as revenue receipts. Revenue receipts include any proceeds from the sale of goods, interest received on deposits, or even dividend on any investments.

Chapter 13.   Debits And Credits

If you're like most people, you probably think of the words "debit" and "credit" in terms of the kind of card you use to pay for items when you go shopping. When you use your debit card, the money comes directly out of your checking account; but when you use your credit card, instead of money being deducted from your bank account, the amount of the purchase is added to the total bill you will pay your credit card company at the end of the month.

This is a very basic understanding of debits and credits can help you navigate the terminology of this part of recording financial transactions for your business. However, in the world of bookkeeping, this essential concept is somewhat more complex.

First, before we explore the specifics of how debits and credits are used to record transactions in bookkeeping, let's consider the basic equation upon which all accounting is based:

Assets = Liabilities + Equity

Whenever you see a mathematical equation, you know that the two elements on either side of the equals sign must have the same numeric value, so the following two equations are correct:

$2 + 1 + 1 = 4$

$3 + 1 = 4$

But this equation is incorrect:

2 + 3 = 4

Because the value of a business is calculated using the accounting equation, Assets = Liabilities + Equity, the numeric values of these terms must be a balanced equation. If they are not, then your business's books are out of balance, and in order to create accurate financial statements, you will have to locate where you have made bookkeeping errors.

Next, before we examine debits and credits in detail, we should take a moment to understand the terms in the accounting equation.

• Assets are any resources that your company owns that represent a future value and can be expressed in monetary value. Cash is one type of asset, but there are many others. For example, investments, inventory, real estate, office supplies, equipment, and accounts receivable, all represent resources that you own and that can be assigned a monetary value. In addition, so-called "intangible assets" include your company's reputation, your client base, the perceived value of your brand, etc.

• Liabilities are the amount of outstanding financial obligations owed by your company. So, your company's liabilities may include the remaining balance on any mortgages, equipment leases, or business loans; accounts payable; or amounts received for future sales that have not yet been delivered.

- Equity is the amount of financial interest all of a company's shareholders have in the company. For example, if you buy 1,000 shares of stock in a new startup company at $2.25 per share, you can personally claim $2,250.00 of that company's value as yours.

So, the accounting equation, Assets = Liabilities + Equity, means that in order for your company's books to be considered balanced and in order, you must be able to show that the total value of all of your assets is exactly equal to the total value of all your liabilities plus the total value of all of the equity all shareholders may have in your company.

This seems like a daunting task, and that's why accounting uses both debits and credits to record transactions.

Importance Of Debit And Credit Accounting

We began this chapter by considering a common understanding of debits and credits – using your debit card takes money out of your checking account; using a credit card adds money to your credit card bill. This is a great start to understanding the importance of using debits and credits to keep accurate books, but in terms of bookkeeping, this concept is more complex.

First, consider the definition of assets above. There are many types of assets, ranging from the balance in your business's main checking account, to the total value of your inventory, to the value of your supplies and equipment, to the value of all the sales you have made for which you are awaiting payment. As a result, an accurate bookkeeping system will need more than just one account to track assets.

Next, you may also have many types of liabilities, including accounts payable and future sales, so you may have more than one account to record all your liabilities.

Finally, in addition to assets, liabilities, and equity, your bookkeeping system will have to keep track of revenue, expenses, gains, and losses.

Taken together, these categories of financial accounts – assets, liabilities, equity, revenue, expenses, gains, and losses – comprise what accountants call the chart of accounts and depending on the size and complexity of your company, the chart of accounts can become fairly complicated.

One more step, and the importance of debits and credits will become clear. Returning to the original example of shopping at your local department store, consider what happens when you buy something with your debit card – the amount of money in your checking account is reduced, but the amount of money in the department store's checking account is increased. In addition, although you have less cash after making the purchase with the debit card, you have increased the value of your assets by the value of the term you purchased; and in return, the value of the store's inventory has decreased by the value of the time they sold. The difference in making the purchase with a credit card is that instead of decreasing the amount of money in your checking account, you increase the amount of money you owe; similarly, the store does not receive an increase in the amount of money in their checking account, but they do see an increase in the value of their accounts receivable.

Thus, the concept behind debits and credits is that every single transaction has two parts – money is taken from one account, and money is added to another account. Because a company's books account for a potentially complex chart of accounts, a system of debits and credits allows the bookkeeper to record all transactions accurately and consistently.

Chapter 14. Recording Debit And Credit In An Account

Figure 3: Free Image

First, remember that in accounting, debit is abbreviated dr. and credit is abbreviated cr. Second, although it is common to associate debit with deducting money and credit with adding money, debits and credits in bookkeeping are used differently.

Depending on which type of transaction the company engages in and which type of account is affected, debits and credits may either increase or decrease the value of any given account. Specifically:

- For asset accounts (e.g., your company's checking account):

o   A debit will increase the value of the account; a credit will decrease the value of the account.

- For liability accounts (e.g., your accounts payable account):

o   A debit will decrease the value of the account; a credit will increase the value of the account.

- For equity accounts (e.g., the shares an investor holds in your company):

o   A debit will decrease the value of the account; a credit will increase the value of the account.

This seems to be the reverse order of the way you may normally think of debits and credits because it is based on the accounting equation, Assets = Liabilities + Equity. Thus, you cannot increase your assets unless you also increase your liabilities or equity. As a result, debits and credits within a bookkeeping system function differently than in a simple check register.

Of course, in some cases, recording a balanced transaction may require increasing the value of one asset account while decreasing the value of another asset account (instead of a liability or equity account). In these cases, there are additional rules that govern the function of debits and credits:

- For revenue accounts:

o   A debit decreases the balance and a credit increases the balance.

- For expense accounts:

o   A debit will increase the balance and a credit will decrease the balance.

- For gain accounts:

o   A debit decreases the balance and a credit increases the balance.

- For loss accounts:

o   A debit will increase the balance and a credit will decrease the balance.

Regardless, in terms of an actual book of accounts, debits are transaction values that are entered on the left side of an account, and credits are transaction values that are entered on the right side of an account.

Third, for every single transaction in bookkeeping, the total amount recorded as a debit must be offset by the exact same amount recorded as credit. If the two sides of the transaction are unequal, the books will not balance, and the bookkeeping system will not accept the entry.

Let's look at some specific examples to clarify the concepts above.

For the first example, let's assume your company sells computer accessories. One of your customers purchases a video camera attachment for a laptop computer at a cost of $375.00. The sale results in an increase in the value of your cash account. It also means that you have increased your revenue by converting inventory into cash. To record this transaction using debits and credits, the bookkeeper will use two accounts: cash and revenue. When you sold the camera attachment to the customer, you received $375.00 in cash, so the cash account is debited for 375. To record the associated increase in revenue, the bookkeeper credits the revenue account for the same amount – 375.

Account	Debit	Credit
Cash	375	
Revenue		375

Alternatively, the records may be displayed as follows:

Cash	
Debits	Credits
375	

Revenue	
Debits	Credits
	375

In the next example, let's assume that your company needs 10 new servers, and each server costs $1,000. You don't want to use your cash account to make this purchase, so you instruct your purchasing agent to buy them on credit. The purchase results in an increase to the value of your fixed assets account. Because they were purchased on credit, there will be an equal increase to the value of your accounts payable. Here is how the bookkeeper will record the transaction:

Account	Debit	Credit
Fixed Assets	10,000	
Accounts Payable		10,000

Again, the same relationship can be displayed as follows:

Fixed Assets	
Debits	Credits
375	

Accounts Payable	
Debits	Credits
	375

Finally, here are some additional guidelines to help get you oriented to the world of debits and credits:

Debit-Credit Table

Account Type	Increase	Decrease
Assets	Debit	Credit
Expenses	Debit	Credit
Liabilities	Credit	Debit
Equity	Credit	Debit
Revenue	Credit	Debit

Debit-Credit Acronyms

The following kinds of accounts (DEAL) are increased with a debit:

- Dividends

- Expenses

- Assets

- Losses

The following kinds of accounts (GIRLS) are increased with a credit:

- Gains

- Income

- Revenues

- Liabilities

- Stockholders' Equity

Debit-Credit Rules

Recording a debit means:

- Increasing the value of an asset account

- Increasing the value of an expense account

- Decreasing the value of a liability account

- Decreasing the value of an equity account

- Decreasing the value of revenue

- Debits are always recorded on the left

Recording a credit means:

- Decreasing the value of an asset account

- Decreasing the value of an expense account

- Increasing the value of a liability account

- Increasing the value of an equity account

- Increasing the value of revenue

- Credit are always recorded on the right

Summary Of Debit And Credit

Double-entry accounting is generally used by businesses because entries always affect at least two different accounts. For example, when a company buys supplies, it affects the cash account and the supplies account or the accounts payable account and the supplies account, depending on if they are paying for the supplies now or in the future.

The double-entry system works using debits and credits. Debits are listed on the left side of the account and credits are listed on the right. Debits increase assets or decrease liabilities, while credits decrease assets or increase liabilities.

It can be tricky to remember which accounts are credited and which are debited. However, there are a few acronyms you can use to remember this information.

Debits increase DEAL accounts, or Dividends, Expenses, Assets, and Losses. These accounts are also decreased by credits.

Credits increase GIRLS accounts or Gains, Income, Revenues, Liabilities, and Stockholders' (Owner's) Equity. These accounts are also decreased by debits.

Chapter 15.   What Is A Financial Statement

Financial statements of the collective term used to refer to a financial report prepared by a business to gauge its financial performance as well as a position at a specific time. Financial statements are prepared with the objective of providing information about the financial health of a business to all those who are interested in the business. It caters to the needs of the investors of creditors, the internal team of management of a business, and also all those other users outside the business. It is the main source of financial information for decision-makers. Apart from this, it also helps check the accuracy and reliability of the books of accounts.

Benefits Of Financial Statements

Financial statements help understand the financial status of a business. The difference between success and failure is based on monitoring the financial health for business. For instance, by properly analyzing the financial statements, you can regulate the way the business spends money and deploy funds towards those activities that are important for the development and growth of the business. In this section, you'll learn about the different benefits associated with financial statements.

The balance sheet provides detailed information on everything that the business owns and owes. The income statement shows the profitability of a business, whereas the cash flow statement covers all finances engaged in business from an accrual to a cash basis. It essentially helps measure the flow of funds in and out of business. So, the first benefit of a financial statement is the provision of a detailed analysis of the financial health of a business.

Since financial statements provide a bird's eye view of the financial position of a business, they are believed to be helpful while making business decisions. They help identify any business trends, the rate at which the businesses are collecting its receivables, any cash flow problems, and the rate of payment of debts. For instance, any report associated with the Accounts Receivable bill helped identify all those who are making timely payments and those who are falling behind on their payments. By using this financial statement, you can determine the list of customers who are in good standing and the ones who are not. Financial statements essentially help with strategic decision-making.

Obtaining credit is an important part of running a business. After all, it is not possible to cater to all the financial requirements of a business from the funds available. Whenever a business applies for a loan, the first thing a lender or a financial institution will look at are the financial statements. A balance sheet shows the creditor all the debts the business has to repay. Apart from this, by maintaining these internal accounts, you can ensure timely and prompt payments of all debts and bills. This, in turn, helps improve the credit standing of the business. Another advantage of preparing financial statements is that they help with tax compliance. To calculate the quarterly state and federal tax obligations, you require financial statements. Sales and annual taxes are state tax obligations. Federal tax obligations include any taxes associated with payroll and annual income. In case of an audit, all these statements come in handy.

Limitations Of Financial Statements

The nature of the figures, along with the way they are reported, usually gives the impression that financial statements are accurate, final, and precise. However, that is not the case. Yes, the statement certainly has a lot of benefits, but there are certain limitations that suffer from too. In this section, let us look at the different limitations of financial statements.

Whatever the profit reported by the income statement and the financial position disclosed by the balance sheet cannot be exact in that since these are just an interim report. The exact position can only be determined whenever the business is liquidated.

The balance sheet is also influenced by various accounting concepts. For instance, fixed assets are always valued by using the going concern concept, whereas detectors and stock in trade are valued using the conservatism concept. Because of this, the balance sheet does not show the financial position of the concern, as it usually claims.

The net income disclosed by the income statement is not always absolute but is relative because the statement is the outcome of different conventions and concepts used, proper recognition of revenue. The concept and conventions affecting the calculation of income are many, the calculation of expired cost is a tricky process, and the recognition of revenue is also affected by different considerations.

Financial statements don't record and reveal any fact that cannot be expressed in monetary terms. For instance, important aspects of a business like the quality of the work done by the employees, the efficiency of the Management, their sales policy, the product or service quality provided by the company, and so on are not exhibited in the financial statements. Anything that cannot be expressed in monetary terms is effectively excluded.

Therefore, keeping in view all these limitations that financial statements are far from, it can be concluded that the statements to the position of financial accounting instead of the financial condition of a business.

Types Of Financial Statements

The four financial statements prepared by every business are as follows.

Income Statement

The income statement is also known as the profit and loss statement. It shows the financial performance of a business in terms of net profit or net loss incurred for a specific period. There are two main elements in an income statement. The first element is the income. It refers to the revenue that the business has during a financial period. The second element is the expense. All the costs associated with running and maintaining the business are included in this portion of the income statement. The balance of an income statement essentially shows whether a business on the profit or sustain the laws during a specific financial period.

Balance Sheet

The balance sheet is also known as the statement of financial position. As the name suggests, it shows the financial position of a business entity at a given time. There are three elements of a balance sheet, and they are the assets, liabilities, and equity. Everything that business owns or possesses a known as its assets..

Cash Flow Statement

The cash flow statement shows the movement of funds between the cash in the bank balances of business over a period of time. There are three aspects of a cash flow statement. These aspects are the operating activities, investing activities, and the financing activities business has undertaken during a specific period. Any cash flow from the primary activity of a business is known as an operating activity. Any cash flow from the purchase or sale of an asset is known as investing activity. Any cash flow associated with obtaining and repaying debts in a business is known as a financing activity.

Statement of Retained Earnings

The statement of retained earnings is also known as the statement of changes and equity. It essentially provides details about the flow of owners' equity in business over a period. This statement is prepared by taking into account net profit or loss, any share capital issued or repaid, payment of dividends, profits or losses arising from changes and equity, and any effect caused because of change in accounting policy or accounting errors.

Chapter 16. Why Do We Need A Financial Statement

The financial statement of a business serves different purposes to a different set of people and the statement is provided for dissemination. There are parts of the financial statement that may be of interest to certain parties as they will divulge that information that helps decision making, checking the status of the company and planning.

In essence, the financial statement provides accounting information about the company, which shows how the business is being run, the way cash and assets are used and what is left after a certain period of time.

The production of financial statements is a collation of bookkeeping for a set period of time. It is expected that a company provides its financial statement to shareholders and the public, so the information provided for that period will be collated and presented. That is why it is important to record every piece of financial information and transactions in an ordered account method for ease in using them to produce such information.

The financial statement is made up of different parts, which provide a different interpretation of how the operation is carried out, the cash flow and how the assets of the company are used.

The income statement is an important financial statement of the company and one that investors are primarily interested in analyzing. From the income statement, the profitability of the Company can be ascertained, as it shows the volume of sale and how the company spends money - that is its expenses. A good income statement shows that the company is healthy and can generate income for investors who will be assured of profit in due time.

The income statement mentioned contains all the expenses the company has operated on over time. With these statements, the person studying the statement can find out the trends within the company. With such knowledge, a decision can be made that will affect the business based on the knowledge of how the company has been spending its cash in their expenses statement.

The balance sheet is another important financial statement that will show the present state of the company at the period the statement was presented. This statement will enable you to analyze the future of the company and if the present way of running the business is sustainable. With this point of view, you can make a decision on how the operation of the business will be handled. From the statement, the liquidity of the business, its funding and debt status of the company can be analyzed. Major decisions affecting businesses can be made when such information is studied.

The statement of cash flow shows the cash movement and the purposes of the operations made. A business owner will want to know the flow of cash and the purposes that cash was used for and how this affects the business. Such statements will determine specific spending in the next business budget. Such statements are important to planning the next business period, after the statement had been produced.

The financial statement contains all major information analyzed, which is a compilation of data recorded over a period of time. All these statements are important for the shareholders, public, investors and for the people running the business.

The aggregates of financial statements are used for:

This can be used by investors to analyze the prices of the business if they intend or are interested in investing in the business. The information is required by the investors as they want to know how the business has been faring over time and determine the profitability of their investments.

Government entities also require the financial statements of a business to estimate the tax or exemption offered to the business. You can calculate your tax returns, which will enable you check for errors by government entities that come to analyze your accounts.

With proper financial statements, you will also be able to check for bank errors, which will save you from paying more than you should pay.

Financial statements are required by lenders to determine if your business is qualified for credit facilities. They will analyze your information to ascertain that the information provided is accurate, which will determine the status of the company to receive credit.

Financial statements provide the public with information on how the business is being operated for a public company.

The financial statement is also essential for internal decision making of the company. The statement, which provides information on how the company is being run, will be used to make future decisions that will affect the business.

The financial statements are a compilation of various information and are used for different purposes depending on who is viewing it.

Chapter 17. Understanding Balance Sheets

The Balance Sheet shows you what the balances in your accounts are at a specific moment in time. The easiest part of this report is that it's set up exactly like the accounting equation! We know that guy by heart by now! :) Assets = Liabilities + Equity.

Below is an example of what Karen's balance sheet looks like before we started helping her. It records all of the information from the beginning of time to the date listed at the top (September 30, 2019.)

Balance Sheet As of September 30, 2019	
ASSETS	
Checking Account 1234	4,921.23
Savings Account 0000	10,468.24
Cash on Hand	550.00
Accounts Receivable	0.00
Total Assets	$15,939.47

LIABILITIES	
Credit Card	399.88
Accounts Payable	0.00
Total Liabilities	$399.88
EQUITY	
Opening Balance Equity	2,561.72
Owner's Investment	1,661.44
Owner's Pay	-5,260.15
Retained Earnings	10,520.30
Net Income	6,056.28
Total Equity	$15,539.59
Total Liabilities + Equity	$15,939.47

As you can see here, the Assets = Liabilities +Equity! It's all shown here as a beautiful report! :)

You may notice that there is an account on here that isn't in our chart of accounts--Net Income.

Net Income isn't an account on it's own. Net Income is the amount the business owner gets when they subtract their expenses from their income. The net income in this report will cover from January 1, 2019 to October 31, 2019. (The net income from all previous years gets lumped together in Retained Earnings.) Each month, the net income will change (brought over from the Profit and Loss report) until the end of the year, when it is moved to Retained Earnings as well. (Don't worry, the main bookkeeping softwares do this for you automatically.)

Let's pretend that we run the Balance Sheet for October 31, 2019 (after we have categorized all of Karen's transactions.) This is what would change, with explanations:

Balance Sheet	
As of October 31, 2019	
ASSETS	
Checking Account 1234	4,921.23 + 547.32 = 5,468.55 (We add the positive difference from the transaction list.)
Savings Account 0000	10,468.24 + 750 = 11,218.24 (We add the money she put in savings.)
Cash on Hand	550.00
Accounts Receivable	0.00
Total Assets	5,468.55 + 11,218.24 + 550 = $17,236.79
LIABILITIES	
Credit Card	399.88 - 134 = 265.88 (We subtract her credit card payment.)
Accounts Payable	0.00

Total Liabilities	$265.88
EQUITY	
Opening Balance Equity	2,561.72
Owner's Investment	1,661.44 + 1,486.49 = 3,147.93 (We add the personal money she put into the business.)
Owner's Pay	-5,260.15 - 1,200 - 1,200 - 116.34 = -7,776.49 (We subtract the two times she paid herself, and also when she bought groceries on accident.)
Retained Earnings	10,520.30
Net Income	6,056.28 + 2,461.17 = 8,517.45 (We add the Net Income from the Profit and Loss report.)
Total Equity	2,561.72 + 3,147.93 +10,520.30 + 8,517.45 - 7776.49 = $16,970.91
Total Liabilities + Equity	265.88 + 16,970.91 = $17,236.79

And there you have it! Now that you know how to do all of this stuff, it's time to try it out for yourself!

Chapter 18.   What To Include In
Balance Sheet Income Statements?

Prepare An Income Statement

An income statement helps report the revenues as well as expenses business has incurred within a specific period. Therefore, it is also known as a profit and loss statement. It is amongst the four major financial statements prepared by a business. It helps determine the profit generated by a business during a specific period. In this section, you'll learn about the ten steps you must keep in mind while preparing an income statement for the business.

Reporting period

Before you can start repairing the income statement, it is quintessential to select the reporting period. A business can prepare its income statement on a monthly, quarterly, or even yearly basis. By preparing a monthly income statement, you can quickly identify any trends in profits as well as the expenditures of your business. This, in turn, can help make better financial decisions associated with the expenditures of the business. By identifying any areas of the business when funds are being constantly drained out from the business, you can take proactive measures to rectify this situation.

Creating a trial balance

Before you can prepare the income statement, you require a trial balance. The trial balance is based on all the balances obtained from the different journals and subsidiary books of accounts prepared during the process of bookkeeping. It essentially gives the balance figures required for preparing the income statement.

Revenue calculation

The next step is to determine the total sales revenue of the business during the period for which the income statement is prepared. The revenue for business includes all the money obtained from services rendered or products sold during a specific period. Even if you haven't received the complete payments yet, all the sales completed will be included. By adding up all the revenue items from the trial balance, you can effectively determine the revenue the business has earned.

Cost of goods sold

The costs incurred in the form of direct labor, materials, and any other overhead expenses included for the provision of goods or services are known as the cost of goods sold. By combining the balance of all these items from the trial balance, you can determine the cost of goods sold in the income statement. This figure will be present directly below the revenue earned in the income statement.

Gross margin

The total revenue minus the cost of goods sold provides the gross margin of the business. This is the gross amount obtained from the sale of goods or services provided by the business.

Operating expenses

All those costs are incurred by a business for the provision of its servers, and day-to-day maintenance of the business operations is included in operating expenses. It includes different expenses such as costs incurred for property taxes, rents, utility costs, advertising costs, entertainment costs, travel costs, and any other amounts payable to employees. Every cost that is directly associated with the day-to-day upkeep of the business is known as an operating expense.

Calculating the income

Once you obtain the gross margin, you must deduct the selling as well as the administrative expenses from it. This provides the income your business has earned. However, keep in mind that this is the income before the payment of different taxes.

Different taxes

Once you have the income payable before income tax, you must make provision for the income tax payable. Calculate the income tax; you merely need to multiply the pre-tax income with the concerned tax rate in the state where the business is located.

Net income

To determine the net income, you must deduct the income tax from the pre-tax income your business is on. This is the final income your business has earned during a specific financial period.

Income statement

To formalize the income statement, you must add a heading identifying the report prepared as an income statement. Once you do this, include all the details associated with the business, and it will provide the income earned during the reporting period.

Income Statement Format

Revenue

(-) Cost of Goods Sold

= Gross Profit or Gross Loss

(-) Operating Expenses (Selling Expenses, Admin Expenses, Depreciation, R&D, And So On)

= Operating Income

Other Income/Expenses

(+) Investment Income

(-) Interest Expense

(-) Taxes Payable

(+/-) Non-Recurring Events

= Net Income or Profit

Understand the Income Statement

Prepare A Balance Sheet

The balance sheet is a financial statement that paints a picture of the financial position of a business. It takes into account the balances of different assets, liabilities, and capital a business has. A balance sheet is always prepared on a specific date for a financial period. A balance sheet is always prepared after the preparation of the trial balance and the income statement. It doesn't include any balances associated with real personal accounts. A balance sheet is prepared on a simple formula.

Assets = liabilities + capital

If this equation is not satisfied, then it is an indication of discrepancies in the books of accounts. A balance sheet must always tally. Let us look in detail about these three components of the balance sheet.

Assets

Anything of value owned by a business is known as an asset. It includes tangible objects as well as intangible assets that are owned by the business. Here are the different types of assets a business can own.

Fixed assets are all those assets that are acquired the higher business for long-term use. These as a not purchased with the intention of resale. Land and buildings, furniture and fixtures, and trademarks and patents, plant, machinery, or anything of a fixed nature that the business owns are all examples of fixed assets.

Floating assets or current assets are those assets present in the business with the intention of being liquidated at the earliest possible. The inventory a business maintains, any amounts receivable from customers, and the bank balances are all included in the category- current assets.

Liquid assets are all those current assets that are already in the form of cash, which can be readily converted into cash like government securities or any existing cash balance.

Wasting assets are certain fixed assets that have fixed content, such as a coal mine. The value of this asset is influenced whenever the contents from it are taken out. For instance, whenever all the minerals from as mine have been extracted, then the mine will be rendered useless.

Intangible assets are those fixed assets that cannot be seen, touched, felt. Goodwill is an intangible asset because even if there is no physical form to it, its effect can be observed in business.

Fictitious assets are those assets that are valueless but are often included in financial statements such as obsolete trademarks or expenses treated as assets. Any expense that is treated as an asset is known as a preliminary expense, and it is often incurred in the process of establishing a business.

Liabilities

Although the financial obligations of a business other than the owner's points are known as liabilities. Essentially, liabilities are all the debts of a business. They include obligations to pay money, obligation to render services, or any other claims against the assets of the business. Here are the different types of liabilities of business might have.

Fixed liability is the term that's collectively used to describe all such liabilities which become payable upon the termination of the liquidation of a business. It includes proprietor's capital and shareholder's funds. Apart from this, there are long-term liabilities like long-term loans from banks that are not payable within a period of one year.

For liability to be classified as a current liability, there are two conditions that must be satisfied. Current liabilities are all such liabilities, which must be repaid within a period of one year. The second condition is that these liabilities must be paid out of current assets. By keeping these two conditions in view, the long-term liabilities due for repayment within one year are termed as current liabilities only when they are expected to be paid out of the current assets of the business. However, any long-term liability that is to be discharged from finances resulting from the issuance of any other long-term liability, then it will not be classified as a current liability. Therefore, examples of current liabilities include short-term loans from banks or bank overdrafts, this payable, outstanding expenses due to creditors, taxes on income, and other amounts payable trade creditors.

Equities

All the claims against all rights in the assets of a business are known as equity is. Equity is a term used to include liabilities to creditors and to the owners of the proprietors of the business. The former is known as critters equity, while the latter is known as owners' equity. Equity refers to any claim that the following people have in a business.

- The claim of an owner

- The claim of a creditor

- The claim of an owner and creditor.

By using this definition of the equity conversed in this section, the following equation can be obtained.

Equity = assets

Shareholder's equity + liabilities = assets

Tips To Prepare A Balance Sheet

Whenever you are preparing a balance sheet, here are a couple of tips you must keep in mind to improve its efficiency.

A balance sheet must always be prepared at the same time every year. This makes it easier to compare the financial performance of the business from one year with the other yours. This, in turn, makes it easier for ratio analysis. If you want to determine whether your business is growing or if it is suffering, then you must be able to make financial comparisons. This is not possible if there is inconsistency regarding the period within which the balance sheet is prepared.

The credibility of the figures you use while celebrating the balance sheet matters a lot. Whenever calculating the value of assets, try to use the current values. Try to be as realistic about these figures as you possibly can. You can either based on values according to the current market values or consider the previous year's values and reduce the same by 5 to 10%. Likewise, you must be consistent and realistic while assessing the real estate value of your business, as well. If these values don't display the true and fair picture, then it fits the purpose of creating a balance sheet altogether.

Chapter 19.   Understanding The Income Statement

An income statement is a financial statement that reflects the profits, losses, income, and expenses of a business during a fiscal period. The income statement is also referred to as a profit and loss statement. The income statement is easy to understand since it states only the revenue and expenses accounts. This financial statement reflects the profitability of a business.

When revenues exceed expenses, the business is profitable. If expenses exceed revenue, the business is running at a loss.

The income statement is a crucial part of a business's financial statements. Used to list the income and expenses, it shows the net income and evaluates the business performance by analyzing non-operating and operating activities.

Investors use the income statement since it provides a clear picture of a business's profitability. This financial statement can influence investor's decisions. The income statements are required from large corporations because they provide users with the necessary details.

Why An Income Statement Is Important

An income statement is important in businesses because of the following reasons:

Reflects the trends and patterns in business's finances. Since income statements are prepared monthly, quarterly, or yearly, companies can use them to compare past income statements with the present one. Comparison analysis can provide a great deal of information regarding the status of the company.

Provides a clear picture of a business's financial position: Income statements help businesses to determine their financial position. With this financial statement, you can easily know if your business is doing well or not.

Helps to make crucial decisions: The income statement is an important financial statement that helps business owners to make critical decisions. If your business is not doing well, you can plan strategies and make decisions that will improve your business's profitability.

Terms Used In Income Statements

Cost of Sales

The cost of sales states the cost of goods sold or services rendered by the business. Depreciation expenses are also included in the cost of sales. For businesses that produce goods, their cost of sales refers to the production of goods. It adds the expenses incurred from purchasing raw materials, labor, and manufacturing.

Retailers and wholesalers are also concerned about the cost of buying and reselling the products. Meanwhile, for businesses that render services, the cost of sales refers to the cost incurred from creating and rendering services to customers.

Net Sales

Net sales are the sales or income of a business. It reflects the sales of goods and services in a specified period. It reflects the profitability of a business.

Income Taxes

The income tax in the income statement is the estimation of income tax for the financial period.

Gross Income

It is also called gross margin or gross profit. The gross income is derived by calculating the difference between the cost of sales and net sales. Gross profit is the money available in a business that can be used to pay off expenses that might be incurred. The greater the gross profit, the more the net income.

Net Income

This is an important aspect of the income statement. The net income lists all operational and non-operational income and expenses and then calculates the difference. When income exceeds expenses, the business is running at a profit; if income is less than the expenses, the business is running at a loss.

Chapter 20. The Cash Flow Statement

The cash flow statement refers to a financial report that states the amount of cash earned and spent in a company. It reveals how cash is moving into and moving out of a business organization. It is also called the statement of cash flow; it is one of the primary financial statements used by financial analysts.

The cash flow statement reflects and evaluates how an organization manages its cash. It reveals how the performance of the balance sheet accounts and income statements influence the flow of cash. Accountants, shareholders, potential investors, analysts, employees, creditors, and contractors are the people interested in the statement of cash flow of an organization.

This financial statement is specifically designed to offer the necessary information on a business's solvency and liquidity. The cash flow statement is primarily concerned about how cash is generated and spent.

The Main Components of the Cash Flow Statement

The cash flow statement is divided into three major components, which are:

The flow of cash from operating activities

The flow of cash from investment

The flow of cash from financing activities

The cash flow statement sometimes adds a disclosure of non-cash activities as part of the components according to the Generally

Accepted Accounting Principles. The cash flow statement is different from the balance sheet account and the income statement.

Cash Flow from Operating Activities

Operating activities involve the manufacturing of goods, sales of goods, receiving payments from customers, and delivering the products of a company. These are activities that generate revenue for a business. These activities have to deal with purchases, sales, and expenses that will generate revenue for the business.

These expenses can be advertising, shipping the goods, purchasing raw materials, and building inventory. Cash flow from operating activities is the cash generated from the income of a company; it excludes costs related to investment in securities or investment on capital items.

The flow of cash from operating activities can be derived by using the direct and indirect method. The direct method reflects how the in-flow and out-flow of cash in the business affect all liability and current asset account. The indirect method reflects how profit is reconciled with cash flow.

Cash Flow from Investing Activities

Investing activities include loans given to suppliers, the sales of assets, purchases of assets, payments linked to acquisitions and mergers, and dividends received from another organization. Cash flow from investment refers to activities that are linked to the sale or purchase of capital assets.

Investing activities refer to activities that generate gain over a long-term period. They lead to changes in non-current assets like equipment, government bonds, investment in shares, etc. Investing activities have nothing to do with cash from external investors like shareholders or bondholders.

For instance, if a company pays out a dividend to its investors, this type of activity is not an investing activity; it is called a financing activity. Examples of investment activities include cash generated from selling an asset, cash spent on the purchase of an asset, cash generated as a result of the merger, cash generated from another company's acquisition.

Cash Flow from Financing Activities

Financing activities refer to events that lead to changes in the composition and size of the capital. Financing activities involve taking out loans, issuance of shares, paying dividends, etc. When a company extends credit to a customer, it is not a financial activity; it is an investing activity.

Cash flow related to repaying loans, borrowing, and issuing of shares is classified as cash flow from financing activities. Financing cash flow reveals the sale or purchase of stock in a company.

How to Calculate Cash Flow

In accounting, cash flow can be calculated by adjusting the net income. The working cash flow is revealed in the statement of cash flow. The working cash flow reflects the in-flow of cash during a particular period. There are two methods of calculating operating cash flow. These methods are direct and indirect.

The direct method derives information from the income statement by making use of cash disbursements and cash receipts. In the direct method, different kinds of payment received and made through cash are added. You can calculate these payments and receipts by making use of the balances of different business accounts.

In the indirect method, working cash flow is calculated by deriving the net income from the income statement of an organization. Because the income statement of an organization is always made on an accrual basis, income is not recorded when it is received; it is recorded when it is earned. The indirect method is not a straightforward method of calculating operating cash flow.

The Importance of Cash Flow Statements

Investors are always concerned about the cash flow of an organization. Positive cash flow is a good sign for investors because this shows that the organization generates cash from its day-to-day operations. Working cash flow can give a clear picture of an organization's profitability.

The purpose of preparing a statement of cash flow is to evaluate the sources of cash and how cash is utilized in a company over a particular period. The cash flow statement is one of the most important financial statements in accounting. Investors depend on this financial statement for making decisions because of its transparency.

The statement of cash flow helps to determine the solvency and liquidity of a business. It provides the necessary details for accessing a company's liabilities, assets, and equity. With the cash flow statement, businesses can determine the trends of their performance. This financial statement also predicts the timing and amount of cash flows in the future.

A business can only be successful if it has enough cash. Cash is needed to make business transactions like paying expenses, paying taxes, purchasing assets, and paying loans. With a cash flow statement, a business can determine the amount of cash available and how cash is generated and spent daily.

A business that lacks enough cash cannot make business transactions, and with time will go bankrupt. Without cash in a business, such businesses will need to borrow money to make some business transactions; this is not healthy for a business. The cash flow is useful in businesses and big organizations.

Chapter 21.   Bottom Line On Financial Statements

These are considered the big four because they are going to give you a good picture of where your business is standing financially. They are also the statements that you need to show your investors to make decisions about whether they will work with you or not. Let's take a look at each one and see how they work and why they are so important for your business.

You must make sure that you fill out these financial statements on a regular basis. Most companies will do one each quarter of their business, and then they do this at the end of the year. There are several benefits to doing this. First, it is required for all publicly traded companies through the SEC. You need to submit these four documents to the SEC at these times to remain on the stock exchange.

You will find that a lot of your investors and lenders will take a look at these financial statements. They are able to get a good view of your financial state and can make smart decisions about whether they want to invest in you or give you a loan. Without this information, the investors and the lenders won't even consider you. So even if the SEC didn't require that you submit this information to them, it could still be useful if you need a business loan to fund something, like new equipment or expansion or to help convince investors that your business is a good option.

Another benefit of using these financial statements is that they give you a good view of your financial statement in the business. You will be able to fill them out pretty easily if you have been keeping good records through the other tips that we talked about. You can then compare this information with the financial statements that you completed in previous quarters and years to let you know the trends of your financial state and make good decisions to prepare you for the future.

Chapter 22.   Choose A Bookkeeping System

There are two recognized systems of GAAP-compliant bookkeeping: single-entry and double-entry. We will explore the pros and cons of both systems in this section. We will also discuss the strengths and weaknesses of online, web-based, and digital bookkeeping systems.

Single-Entry Bookkeeping

A single-entry bookkeeping system is the most informal of all bookkeeping systems. If you have a checking account, the check register is a great example of single-entry bookkeeping. All the transactions in the check registry provide information about only the one checking account. Whether the transaction is a deposit resulting for a business transaction; from a personal or professional investment; from a business or personal loan; or from interest paid on the account or dividends received from investments in securities, all the transactions are listed chronologically, with a small space for description of the transaction, and a column on the right to show how the transaction affected the balance in the account.

Withdrawals are tracked the same way – whether a withdrawal results from a direct withdrawal from the bank for personal or business use; for payment of a bill for operating expenses for your business; form a purchase made for equipment or office supplies; from payments for loans, interest, or taxes; or from the purchase of investments, all the transactions will be listed chronologically; again with a small space for a description of the transaction; and a column on the right to show how the transaction affected the balance.

This method of bookkeeping is fairly straightforward and can be an effective means of showing accurately where money comes in and goes out each month. However, with the prevalence of online banking, we have all encountered the difficulty of keeping track of all transactions in a simple check register. Previous top widespread access to online banking, most deposit transactions were made in person at the bank, and most withdrawals were conducted by mailed checks. This level of control over financial activity made the single-entry system a more viable option for individuals and businesses over a much broader range of business contexts. The contemporary environment requires a reassessment of whether a single-entry system is right for you.

Advantages:

- Single-entry bookkeeping uses a simple and easy-to-understand method of keeping track of transactions.

- Small businesses that have only one major financial account may be able to save time and expense by using this system effectively.

- A single-entry system can be adapted for larger companies by creating separate single-entry systems for each business account.

Disadvantages:

- Single-entry systems do not provide a means of including detailed financial reporting.

- Bookkeeping errors can be very difficult to locate and usually involve reconciling bookkeeping records with bank statements.

- Single-entry systems do not provide an effective means of creating projections of future financial performance.

- Single-entry systems generally track only cash accounts. Other assets, as well as liabilities, equity, income, and expenses go unreported in these systems.

Double-Entry Bookkeeping

Especially in a globalized, digital environment, it is common even for small, local businesses to have many accounts with different suppliers, service providers, and customers, often from different locations and even different countries. In addition, the increasingly self-service nature of investing and business administration can mean that even small businesses may have to take on considerably greater responsibility than in previous eras. Regardless, the larger and more complex your business, the more likely a double-entry system will allow you to consistently maintain reliable books. Most companies use the double-entry system.

In the section above, we used the analogy of a check register to describe the single-entry system. Using a double-entry system, the transactions in the previous example represent only half of the entire bookkeeping process. For example, if you made a deposit into your checking account for payments received from customers for good and services sold, the record of the deposit into the checking account (a single-entry) is only half of the transaction record; in order to balance the books, there needs to be a second-entry is a corresponding account. The idea behind double-entry systems is that putting money into one account necessarily means that money was taken from another account and vice-versa. Double-entry bookkeeping allows you to show both sides of the transaction. So, when a company makes a deposit resulting from sales, revenue can be credited for the same amount the checking account was debited, which results in a balanced record of the transaction. Similarly, if the business owner pays an outstanding bill for shipping, the double-entry system will record a credit to the checking account and a debit to the accounts payable.

Advantages:

- Provides a more complete system of recording all of a company's financial transactions, not just deposits and withdrawals to the main checking account.

- Provides a means of producing accurate and reliable financial statements.

- Provides an effective means of pinpointing internal accounting errors.

- Provides a means of accurately assessing a company's financial condition.

Disadvantages:

- Double-entry bookkeeping is more complex and may take more time to learn.

Chapter 23. Choose An Accounting Method: Cash Or Accrual

Cash-Based Accounting

Under this accounting system, you only record revenue/income and expenses whenever there is an actual exchange of cash. You only record expenses and purchases when you have paid cash for them and income when a customer has paid for the goods/services.

For instance, if Mr. A buys a product or receives a service from you in January but does not pay for it until May, you would have to wait until May when Mr. A pays for it before you record the transactions.

Benefits of Cash-Based Accounting

Using the cash-based system of accounting has some advantages:

Very simple and uncomplicated such that you can easily handle your bookkeeping with zero accounting knowledge/experience.

You don't need complex software or accounting records; oftentimes, all you need is your check booklet.

Naturally, everything that has an upside also has a downside:

Downsides of Cash-Based Accounting

Cash-based accounting is not always advisable to use because it provides insufficient records and does not really provide a true and clear picture of what is really going on in the business. For instance, you could erroneously report that your business made losses in January because you were yet to receive payments for the products/services sold.

Cash-based accounting also focuses on revenues and expenses alone and ignores other aspects of the business such as assets, inventory, liabilities, equity, and so on.

It also does not conform to the generally accepted accounting principles (GAP) or international financial reporting standards (IFRS).

Which Types of Businesses can Use Cash-Based Accounting System?

Legally, only a few businesses have the green light to use the cash-based system of accounting. You can use cash-based accounting if your business falls within any of the following categories:

Sole proprietorship with annual average gross receipts of less than $1,000,000

S-Corporation with annual average gross receipts of less than $1,000,000

C-Corporation with annual average gross receipts of less than $5,000,000

A company not publicly traded or not under any obligation to make full disclosure to the IRS

Family-owned farms with annual gross receipts of less than $25,000,000

Accrual Based Accounting

Under the accrual based accounting system, you record transactions when earnings are made and expenses are incurred, not when they are paid for.

In this case, dollar bills or checks do not have to exchange hands before you record such transactions; every time a transaction occurs, you have to record it in your books.

For example, let's assume YXL Ltd. hires you to repair some of its equipment in January and you charge them $5,000 for this service. However, YXL Ltd. does not issue a check immediately but promises to discuss it with the financial accountant and then get back to you. This system of accounting requires that you record this transaction in your accounts receivable books as soon as you complete the job whether YXL makes payments for it or not.

There are two major account items you have to record when using the accrual method of accounting:

Accounts Receivable: Account receivable would include all the monies owed to your business not paid.

In this example, as soon as you send out your invoice for the sales of a product or service, you record the value in your accounts receivable ledger.

This account helps you track everything owed to your business.

Accounts Payable: Account payable is the exact opposite of accounts receivable. Here, you record all the monies your business owes to other people.

As soon as you receive an invoice or make a commitment to the other party, you have to record the transaction in your account payable book so you can track what your business owes to other people.

Benefits of Accrual Based Accounting System

Using the accrual based system of accounting has many benefits.

For starters, the accrual based accounting system produces a more accurate and reliable accounting report, and gives a true and clear picture of the performance of the business.

It also provides a basis for comparing your accounting results.

Downsides of Accrual Based Accounting System

This method of accounting is usually harder and more complicated than the cash based method of accounting where you only need to record cash transactions.

Which types of Businesses Should Use Accrual Based Accounting System?

Use the accrual based accounting system if your business is:

A C-corporation

Your business has inventory

You are obligated by the IRS to make full disclosure of your business.

Your business has gross sales revenue that is higher than $3million every year.

Chapter 24.   Organize And Store Your Documents

A lot of entrepreneurs struggle with bookkeeping and maintaining a record of financial transactions. According to a survey, only 40% of small business entrepreneurs feel that they have the required in-depth knowledge of bookkeeping and business accounting. Which brings us to the next point: being a successful business owner is not equivalent to being a successful bookkeeper.

However, effective bookkeeping is the key to a successful and thriving business. This is why most business owners either learn bookkeeping and implement it by themselves or hire accounting firms or professional bookkeepers to do it for them. To be good at business, you need to be good at money-making. Running a business smoothly requires years of tried and tested strategies, a disciplined and organized mindset, and a lot of expertise.

Running a business with accounting loopholes hinders its productivity and success rate. This is where the implementation of good bookkeeping practices proves its significance. It is imperative to a business that it employs the best strategies, the most effective tools, and regular account management practices to run smoothly and successfully.

Understand The Importance Of Keeping Accurate Financial Records

For this purpose, it is best to work with a team. The responsible parties must know and be trained to keep accurate financial records effectively. It is significant for a business owner to realize the importance of keeping accurate and updated financial records because eventually, it relies on them to implement the best bookkeeping practices within their organization.

When financial reports are due for a review by the management team, the records should be ready and updated. Mapping out a schedule for this purpose could prove to be crucial in ensuring that the financial data is reviewed on time and routinely to identify the trends in the business' cash flow.

Only when a business owner is well-informed of the trends, status, and cash flow of their business will they be able to make informed and effective decisions.

Keep Track Of Profits And Expenditures

Records of profits and expenditures of your business are the essential information listed in your book. You can note it in a diary or a ledger to document your credit and debit activities. To record profits, you must maintain an Accounts Receivable column in your ledger and note down the money you are to receive from your clients.

It is imperative to keep an updated record of your profits and expenditures. Maintaining updated records of the money your business spends and that it earns helps you stay in the loop about the progress of your business and determine its success rate.

If You Are Not Ready – Outsource

Bookkeeping is a tedious and time-consuming process. So if you feel like it is not something you particularly like doing, or think you are not good at it, it is better to outsource your accounts to independent accounting firms or hire a professional bookkeeping service to handle your financial records. Keeping bookkeeping records, especially when you run a large-scale business, is challenging.

Most large-scale business owners tend to outsource their books because they feel spending time on bookkeeping is keeping them from money-making and being more productive for their business. As a result, a lot of entrepreneurs leave bookkeeping to professional bookkeepers and accountants or outsource it to a firm specialized in maintaining accounts.

On the other hand, a lot of small business owners tend to do their own bookkeeping. It saves them a lot of money and time because

1. Their financial records are comparatively precise and not as extensive as those of large businesses

2. Doing their own bookkeeping keeps them in the loop and enables them to make decisions that could their business grow.

However, as the business grows, entrepreneurs prefer to spend their time making more sales instead of maintaining the books. Sometimes, you make errors in bookkeeping. Fixing those errors requires time most business moguls don't have. Therefore, in lieu of doing their own bookkeeping, they hire proficient accounting firms to handle the accounts for their businesses.

Always Be On The Lookout For Business Apps

Business apps are specially integrated with different accounting software packages to give you improves results and assist you in bookkeeping. It takes these apps only a fraction of the time it may take you to perform these tasks manually. For instance, a time tracking app allows you to maximize your work potential and increase profitability without having to go to great lengths and implement procedures that would enable you to do so.

Business apps that provide you feedback regarding your billing hours and more valuable data are the most resourceful. They allow you to draft future proposals, bill clients, verify vendor bills, and evaluate what works for your business and what does not.

Maintain Accurate Documentation Of Inventory

Inventory management is an elementary part of a business, especially small businesses that need to maintain an accurate record of all inventories to cease overproduction, product misplacement, and stealing. Maintaining your inventory holdings allow you to keep track of sales trends and devise your business strategies by analyzing these trends.

Keeping an accurate record of your inventory helps you maintain information about stock statistics, purchase and sales costs, and dates purchased. Updated documentation of your inventory will keep you informed of the figures and enable efficient decision-making regarding merchandise.

Document Your Purchases

Any material, whether raw or processed, you buy for your business must be mentioned in the books to keep track of your purchases. It is an important part of running a business and helps you determine your company's sales and profits.

Eventually, every business, through trial and error, develops a method of bookkeeping that works for them and does the job efficiently. The entire process of getting there, however, requires the implementation of effective and advanced techniques that would enhance your accounting methods, add to your expertise, make business handling easy, and provide room for the business to grow.

If you find documenting your purchases and keeping your books updated difficult and time-consuming, you can always hire the services of outsourcing account companies to handle your company's bookkeeping on your behalf.

Do Not Overlook Account Reconciliation

Account reconciliation is one of the most important yet neglected tasks on this list. It allows you to look over all financial transactions and ensure you have fully accounted for everything. It helps you restore order to hurried, haphazard bookkeeping, and review all financial details.

In addition to reconciling your bank accounts, you should also conclude it with an ending balance. This should apply to all business accounts, credit and debits, payroll liabilities, loans, and more. The best way to do account reconciliation is to go through your finances every day. Waiting till the end of the month will add to your workload, so try doing daily reconciliations.

Use Bookkeeping To Grow Your Business

If you have mastered even half of these strategies, you are already hitting all the right places with your bookkeeping. In that case, it is time to take your bookkeeping to the next level. You can take your bookkeeping practice and turn it into an effective tool to grow your business.

It is time you take these reports and perform an analysis to see how it could help your business grow and prosper. Once you have performed the analysis, it is time to draw some conclusions, prepare reports, have your team members deliver their reports to you, and observe the pattern it incorporates into your business. You can then use these trends to further your business, hit some major goals, achieve milestones, and prepare yourself for the future.

A lot of businesses want to know if they need improvement, what areas need to do better, and how to go about doing it. But they have no way to determine if they are doing well. For this purpose, you can review your financial reports, develop a budget, and then compare your business' performance to the set budget. There is no way to determine if your business is doing well when you don't have the goals to measure up against it.

Categorize Your Expenses

Categorizing makes everything simpler and easier. Putting your expenses into categories will make it easier and faster for you to keep a record of your company's finances. It will also make your bookkeeping neat and more efficient.

Sometimes it takes business owners years to realize the importance of sorting their expenses into relevant categories. Each year they file different expenses under different labels, and then they have to sort through years of expenses to do everything correctly. Categorizing the money your business has spent will make it easier for you to sort through the books later.

If You Outsource Your Accounts – Don't Be Hands-Off

Outsourcing your books and getting it done by a hired professional does not mean you should completely overlook your responsibility in bookkeeping. Since you are the business owner, it would be ideal if you would do the bookkeeping by yourself. But running a large enterprise and doing its bookkeeping is a handful.

So, as mentioned before, most large business owners outsource their books. But they still must take ample interest in their company's financial records. They must have a look through them once a month, or maybe on alternative months, or quarterly basis – whichever works for them. It is imperative for the owner of the company to be fully aware of the numbers. It helps them determine the financial standing of the company, which includes profits, losses, payables, receivables, etc.

They can work alongside their accountant to determine their future business goals and how to achieve them.

Keep A Tab On The Receivables

Invoice raising and timely collection is a sign of a good account receivable. Working efficiently ensures effective cash flow in the company. You must maintain a record of all the invoices, their terms of payment, and if you paid them completely or just partially.

Receivables are not just about receiving payment. They are to hold you accountable for the money coming into the business and to make sure no payment is released without a proper invoice.

Always Create Backup Archives For Bookkeeping Files

Never leave your bookkeeping files without a backup. Either set up an automated backup or run regular backups to have your files saved in case of a system crash. Mishandling the files, system failure, and other possibilities can lead you to lose a lot of important financial evidence and account statements, which is why it is always recommended to create a backup of your bookkeeping records.

You must always create at least 2 to 3 duplicates or more of your books. This way, you can have your records stored in different hard drives or memory devices. If an incident such as a system crash does occur, you will always be able to retrieve your bookkeeping files. A printed copy works even better. It will give you a paper trail of all accounting records and will make it easier for you to catch up on your transactions without taking too much time.

Self-Audit As Much As You Can

Self-auditing will save you a lot of trouble in the long run. It is best to look over your accounts and take note of all your accounting loopholes and bookkeeping errors by self-auditing before doing anything else. Once every month, sit with your books, sift through your financial transaction, meticulously check each entry, and determine if anything needs to be altered or if something is missing from the books.

This will keep you in the loop about your business' finances and help you rectify errors. This practice will also prevent your business from encountering any discrepancy or suffer through an accounting setback. Before going for help to any bookkeeping expert or seeking help from professional bookkeeping services, self-audit and look over the financial transactions by yourself.

Keep Personal Transactions And Business Transactions Separate

People owning a small business tend to mix often personal and business accounts. This is one of the most important problems to be considered because putting in single entries for both personal and business transactions is a financial debacle. It will be confusing when you will later go over the books and have a hard time differentiating one finance from the other.

It is best that you maintain separate accounts for both personal and business transactions. Opening a separate bank account and keeping separate books and statements for your business and personal expenditure will help you run your business effectively.

Choose The Right Bookkeeping Software

One of the most effective strategies is to pick the right bookkeeping software. It should be your first priority to pick the software that is suitable for the size of your business, the relevant industry, and your financial data. It is not as extensive or difficult to find the right software. The purpose of bookkeeping software is to make your life a little easier and make the process less tedious and tiring. You must select the software that automates and optimizes you're your entries and makes keeping financial records simple.

For business owners, especially those who do their own bookkeeping, time is of the essence. They must carefully pick effective tools that would help save their time, energy, and make handling the finances efficiently. When looking for the software, you must take its skill, technical ability, and features into account.

Bookkeeping software should provide the following results:

• Must manage multiple clients and businesses using a single login

• The software must fit all your requirements

• Must save time and make bookkeeping efficient

• Should be smart, quick, and easy to use

• It must provide Cloud-based access everywhere

• Must allow easy sharing of MIS reports

Make Timely Payment of Bills

Ignoring your bills is tempting, but leaving them unpaid is not a strategic bookkeeping move. The longer you wait, the more unpaid amounts assemble, and the worse it gets for you to keep a record of all your unpaid dues. Irrespective of whether it is a credit charge or a late fee, make sure always to make your payments on time.

In the long run, the amounts you have left unpaid will hurt your bookkeeping practice as well as your business. The longer you wait, there will be more unpaid charges due to the rate of interest. All in all, in the end, you will have a huge bill to pay with added charges, interest, and arrears charges. If you are handling your business alone, it can be difficult for a single individual to pay everything at once.

Precaution is always good, but what's better is to be punctual with your payments. To avoid any unnecessary trouble, keep clearing your bills from time to time.

The aforementioned strategies are simple steps that will maximize your business' effectiveness, help you grow your business, save time, and make bookkeeping easy for you. When handling your company's records, it is always best to team up with someone to go over the books once. Sometimes, another set of eyes picks up on errors one may overlook.

On the other hand, if you are not handling your books and have hired a professional service to do it, you must always schedule reviews with your bookkeeper to have a clear understanding of your business and learn of its potential to grow.

Chapter 25. Organize Potential Deduction

When you file income tax at the end of the year, you should be able to deduct the expenses associated with running your business from the total revenue earned. When you report a lower total revenue, you will be less in taxes. The following are the types of business expenses the IRS allows you to deduct on our tax returns:

● Business start-up costs. The types of costs associated with start-ups vary depending on the type of business but may include:

○ advertising

○ travel

○ surveys

○ training

○ asset purchases

● Depreciation. If you purchased assets that will last longer than one year, you can claim as start-up expenses. However, you can claim the value of depreciation for such assets. Typically, asset depreciation is claimed for the following types of assets:

○ office furniture

○ buildings

o   equipment and machinery

- Business use of home. If your home is your principal place of business, you may be able to claim certain tax deductions, but you will have to provide documentation that shows:

o   what business services are performed at your home.

o   how your home has been converted to business use.

- Car and truck expenses. Keeping accurate records of your car and truck usage can also help you find ways to save money. The following types of business-related travel expenses are deductible:

o   depreciation

o   lease payments

o   registration

o   garage rent

o   licenses

o   repairs

o   gas

o   oil

o   tires

o   insurance

o   parking fees

o   tolls

Chapter 26.   Comon Bookkeeping Pitfalls To Avoid

Mistake #1- Not Reconciling Your Accounts

Reconciling is the process of matching your transactions in QuickBooks with a source document- usually a bank or credit card statement.

This simple function is the way you make sure the balances you are seeing in your books actually match with reality. The longer you go without reconciling, the more likely it is the books are off- maybe way off, depending on how you do things.

One of the very first things we check with any new client is whether the books have been reconciled correctly or not. If the answer is no, 99% of the time there are mistakes in the books we have to find and fix.

Mistake #2- Not Using Sales Tax Correctly

Sales tax is a little bit of a tricky concept in accounting because although you get the money, you handle the money, and you deal with the money - it isn't yours. So you need to account for it as though it isn't and not lump it in with the rest.

The problem is the sales tax funds are mingled right in with your funds and it all looks the same. If you are creating invoices and collecting sales tax that way, it is easier to keep it straight. Make the appropriate items taxable and make sure when you pay your sales tax, you are reducing the sales tax liability account. There are lots of lessons online on how to do this correctly

Mistake #3- Not Handling Loans Correctly

More than half of all small businesses have at least one loan of some kind that they need to track, but very few of them are set up correctly.

These could be loans to start the business, a loan for a car, a loan for equipment or even an SBA loan to buy the business in the first place.

No matter what it is for, all loans have several parts to them, most of which get skipped. In fact, there is the loan beginning balance, the principle repayment and the interest expense that need to be accounted for in the books.

Mistake #4- Not Using Invoicing Right

There are two common mistakes (and then lots of less common - but still problematic - mistakes) people make with invoices, although invoices themselves are pretty simple.

An invoice is a request for payment for products or services or both. The trick with invoices is that as soon as you create one, it counts as income, even if you haven't been paid a cent.

Mistake #5- Not Doing Payroll Right

Paying payroll is one of the basic functions of having a business for a lot of business owners but it is also one of the more misunderstood aspects of small business.

The first mistake people make is calling things payroll that aren't. Unless you take payroll taxes and withholdings from a checkand the person you are paying is an employee of yours and has given you a W-4 form, the check isn't a paycheck. Lots of payments to people get called paychecks that aren't actually paychecks. Maybe they should be, but they aren't!

Mistake #6- Not Tracking 1099s

1099s are issued to individuals or companies that provided you with services during the course of the year that added up to $600 or more in total payments. Employees and corporations are exempt, as are product purchases. Some LLCs are exempt. Law firms are normally not exempt. The rules start to get a little tricky and change a bit every year on who qualifies.

Mistake #7- Not Using Assets Correctly

Assets have specific definitions in accounting, but most people don't realize what they are and this is where mistakes happen. Most people think of assets simply as "things I have" but that doesn't get specific enough for accounting.

Mistake #8- Not Using Equity Right

Equity represents your ownership in your business. It is the section that comes after liabilities and just before income in the chart of accounts.

Chapter 27. Loan Payments

Most sellers start using their own money but occasionally someone will get money from a friend or relative to start the business or to buy inventory or something. Or, they may borrow funds against a car, house or get credit from a vendor.

In these cases you want to record the amount you got and also any repayments you make or interest you pay.

Let me start with an investment first because It is easier. If someone gives you money to start or grow your business and they are not going to be getting paid back on an agreed schedule or if they explicitly are buying part ownership in the business then you will use an equity account. When you record the deposit for the money they give you, the account it goes to is an equity type account. Whether they are a partner, member or shareholder depends on the type of entity you have.

Whichever it is, make sure you record every time they put money in so you have a running total of their investment. If they are coming on as a partner, make sure you have a partnership agreement in place and everyone is crystal clear on roles, responsibilities, profit sharing future partnerships, etc. before you take a dime.

If the money coming in is a loan, then when you record the deposit the account it goes to is a liability account. If you expect to pay it back in a year or less, it is a current liability. If you expect it to take a year or more, then it is a regular liability.

When you start making payments back, if you are paying interest then be sure to split each payment into the principal portion and the interest portion and record the amount going to each account. The principal portion should go to the original loan account to reduce the balance. The interest portion goes to an interest expense account and is a tax deduction.

For example, if you are making a loan payment of $225 you might have $200 going to reduce the balance $25 going to interest. If the total loan amount was $2000, in ten payments you will have paid off the loan and also paid $250 in interest.

The mistake most people make with loans is they record the loan payments but they never recorded the original balance. Or they do not split the interest. Or worst of all they record the original loan deposit as income and then it looks like you owe income tax on money that was a loan! If you need help here, just ask us!

Paying Yourself & Others

How you get paid by the business depends on what type of entity you are operating. If you are a sole prop, the money in the business is your money whether you take it out or leave it in the bank.

You can transfer it as needed to your personal account to spend on personal stuff but if your business is making money be sure to set aside a good chunk to pay taxes. As a sole proprietor you are also going to charged self-employment tax which means you are going to be paying the government for Social Security and Medicare and a few other things and not just the portion that would normally come out of a paycheck but also the portion that the employer would normally pay. This adds up to be about 15% of your total profit!

So for example, if the business makes $50K as a sole proprietor you are going to pay $7500 in self-employment tax aside from any state or federal income tax you might owe!

If you are an LLC you make take your money in the form of profits and/or guaranteed payments. Again, you are going to end up paying self-employment tax on this money in addition to income tax.

If your LLC is set up to be taxed as an S Corp, or you are an S Corp, then once the business starts to make some money you can put yourself on payroll. For the amount you take as payroll, you are also going to be paying the self-employment taxes (half as the employee and half paid by the corporation which is also essentially you!). But, with a corp, you can also take money out as a distribution, which is payroll tax free!

This is one of the big savings you can get from a tax perspective as an S Corp or LLC taxed as one. You can pay yourself a smaller amount of payroll and take the larger portion of your income as distributions.

In the example above, if the business made $50,000, you could take $20,000 as salary and pay $3,000 in payroll taxes and the other $30,000 in distributions and pay no payroll taxes. In that case you have saved yourself $4,500 in taxes!

The catch is you must set up payroll and pay payroll taxes and file your payroll tax forms and in all ways be a legitimate employer paying payroll. This does take some time and work and effort if you do it yourself. If you would like help, we can do this for you as well!

The other catch is you must pay yourself a "reasonable" salary if you are active in the business and the business is profitable. The government does not define what reasonable is so It is up to you. The good news is, because an Amazon business does not require much labor or time, you can pay yourself something fairly low and still make a reasonable argument It is a fair wage for the time and energy you are putting in.

Now, aside from payroll there is one other kind of payment we should discuss that is related to payroll but not the same.

Paying 1099 Vendors

1099s are issued to individuals or companies in the US that provided you with services during the course of the year that added up to $600 or more in total payments. Your own employees and corporations you do business with are exempt, as are product purchases. Some LLCs are exempt, but most are not. Law firms are normally not exempt. The rules start to get a little tricky and change a bit every year on who qualifies.

But you can be well ahead of the game if you make a point of tracking who you are doing business with, considering if they may qualify for a 1099 and if so, requesting they provide you with a completed W-9 form.

The best way to get vendors to comply is to hold their payment until they provide you with the form. Since it only takes about 10 seconds to fill out, most people will get it for you immediately if it means they get their check.

If someone insists they will not allow you to issue them a 1099, then you have a decision to make. If you do not issue a 1099 to someone who is eligible, and still claim the expense (hey- I did pay him!) then you potentially run the risk of not being allowed to use that expense if your tax return is audited.

Issuing a 1099 is your proof you paid for the service and that the government should look for income taxes from that person, not you. If you do not issue the 1099, the government can claim the payment never got made (or you wrote a check but they turned around and cashed it and gave you the cash back), and therefore you owe income tax on the amount that expense was used to lower your net profit.

The reason this is an issue is because each year, 1099s are due to be filed by January 31st. But you will not have final payments made until (maybe) the end of December. So by the time the books are done for December, you may only have a week or less to get all your 1099 info together and filed. If your books are not done, or you do not have your 1099 vendors identified ahead of time, it may not get done at all.

This is easy to do right from the start and a pain to catch up later. Yet very, very few of the clients we have were doing this correctly when they were doing it themselves or even when paying someone else to do it.

Go through your list of active vendors and identify which ones are eligible for a 1099. If you do not have a W-9 on file for them, ask them for one now – before you issue them another payment. Mark their account as 1099 eligible in QB.

Some will take longer to get than others and some might not make it to $600, but for those who do, your job will be vastly easier and you will be on the right side of the IRS when you can easily issue 1099s to everyone who gets one well ahead of the January 31st deadline.

Chapter 28. Inventory Count

Inventory Value

If a company purchases raw material and spends more of its funds doing this, then there will be an increase in the inventory. If the inventory was acquired using cash, then any increase in the value of the inventory will be deducted from the net sales of the company. Likewise, any decrease in the inventory will be added to the net sales. There will be an increase in accounts payable if the inventory was purchased on credit, and the same will be reflected on the balance sheet. The amount of increase from one year to the other in inventory levels will be added to the net sales. The same criteria are used for taxes payable, prepaid insurance, and any salaries payable. If an expense has been paid off, then the difference between the value owed from one year and the next must be subtracted from the net income. If there is an outstanding amount, then any differences need to be added to the net earnings.

Inventory Buffers

It is extremely important to maximize the capacity in a constrained operation every time. One of the best ways to do it is by building an inventory buffer in front of the constraint operation. This inventory buffer will assure that any shortage of production of any parts of the operation will not hamper the continuous process or production of the product and it usually fluctuates in size as it gets used and replenished.

The performance of a company can improve by installing a sprint capacity in the production areas of the company.

Sprint Capacity

Sprint capacity is an increasingly high amount of production volume that is amassed in the factories or workspaces. When a mishap happens in the factory, and it cannot be avoided, the continuous flow of parts is stopped, and that's when sprint capacity is required. In this phase, the bottleneck takes resources from inventory buffer, which ends up in shortage in inventory buffer. So extra sprint capacity is required to mass-produce parts to refill the parts shortage in inventory buffer so that it can be used in the next unavoidable mishap.

It's a wise decision to invest in a large sprint capacity in a production company as it can rebuild the inventory buffer is a short span of time. So, if you can invest in a large sprint capacity, only a small investment is required for investment buffer. Or else if you invest in large inventory buffer, there will be less sprint capacity.

One of the main points we can learn here is that it is always a better option to maintain some space in the capacity in work areas and not limit the production capacity to the current needs.

Chapter 29. Bookkeeping Tips For Small And Medium Business

As a new entrepreneur, you have a lot of financial details that you have to keep track of to help the business run efficiently. Doing this well has a lot of advantages. It can help you to make sure that you are making profits and understand exactly where your money is going each month. It helps you to be prepared for tax season at the end of the year. And it can ensure that you are paying your employees properly and that your business is growing the way that you want.

Getting started with bookkeeping may seem a bit confusing when you first get started. There are many different forms that you need to pay attention to, and this can be scary for a lot of beginners who have never experienced these before. Let's look at some of the best bookkeeping tips that you can follow to help your business stay financially secure.

Plan For The Major Expenses

There are times when a big expense is going to come up. If you don't plan for these issues, you will either put yourself in trouble with money, miss out on some big opportunities, or have to go out with something. When you plan for these major expenses, and they are going to show up at some point, you will either have to miss out on a business opportunity that is important to you, or you may have to scramble for a loan from the bank if you have to pay. For example, if your computer system crashes and you need to pay for some IT to come in, it is much better to have this money on hand rather than scrambling to get a loan and get it fixed in time.

There are several things that you can do when this happens. First, put big events, computer upgrade that is needed, on the calendar a year in advance. If you can, write this down every year for the next three to five years. You can also acknowledge on the calendar some of the periodic ups and downs the business has and make sure that you are putting enough money aside to make it through these leaner months as well.

Often the costly things that you need to fix are going to show up in the easier months for your company. Do you really want to get caught in the trap of taking out money during the busy periods, just to find out that you are short on money for major repairs in some of the slower months?

Track All The Expenses

You want to keep accurate records of all the expenses and transactions that come up with your business. Tracking these not only give you a good idea on how the finances of the business are doing, but it can help you with tax season. If you don't keep good track of the expenses that you take on during the year, you might miss some tax write-offs or have to give up on a few because you just don't have the right information.

Having the right bookkeeping methods in place, and keeping all the receipts of your business along the way, can help you out here. You should either have everything added and uploaded to your online bookkeeping software or have another system of accounting that you can work with to help keep everything organized. This will go a long way in helping you see results.

This means that you should keep track of everything that you do with your business and every expense that you take for the business. This includes any events that take cash, any coffee dates, lunches, and business trips, should be kept track of. This habit is going to go a long way in the direction of substantiating those items for your tax accounts in case you are audited. These records make sure that you are safe in case the IRS wants to look at your records and can make it easier to know what tax deductions you get in the first place.

Record The Deposits Correctly

The best thing here is to take up a system that will keep all the financial activities of your business straight, whether it is a notebook that you use on a regular basis, the help of an Excel spreadsheet, or some software that can record all your financial information.

Being a business owner, you need to make a wide variety of deposits into your bank account throughout a fiscal year, including deposits about revenue from any sales, cash infusions from the personal savings, or loans. The trouble here is that when the year ends, you (or a bookkeeping you decide to work with), might go through this information and then record some of the deposits as income when they aren't your income. And when this happens, you could end up paying taxes on more money than what you actually made that year.

Set Money For Your Taxes

If you are past the first year of business, or you are a sole proprietorship who owed the IRS $1,000 or more for a year, then you need to file quarterly tax returns. If you fail to do this, then the IRS could levy interest and penalties for not filing these on time.

The best thing to do is to systematically put some of the money aside during the year that you can use to pay your taxes. Then, on the calendar, you will note the deadlines for the taxes, along with any preparation time if it is needed. This ensures that you are actually able to make the tax payments to the IRS on time when they are due.

One thing that can be especially problematic for your business is payroll taxes. There are times when some entrepreneurs, who aren't taking care of their finances properly, will be crash-crunched and end up in a down cycle. They will dip into the employee withholdings, the money that was earmarked to be sent to the IRS.

If you start messing with these payroll taxes, you are going to end up with a twofold problem. First, you haven't paid the taxes that are due for the employees, and you have taken money that the IRS sees as belonging to the employees. The IRS is not going to be very happy about this situation, and you will end up in a lot of trouble. Set aside some money to help you pay your quarterly taxes.

Keep A Tab On The Invoices That You Have

You will quickly find in your business that any late bills or unpaid bills are going to cut into the cash flow that you have. When people are not paying the invoice that they owe to you, and you had to pay for employees to do the work and materials, this can really end up putting you behind. You had to pay for everything upfront, and now you have to make due and keep getting things paid upfront for other customers, without having that money from the original customers.

You have to always keep track of the invoices that you have to make sure they are all paid on time.. Then put a process in place so that you can make phone calls, send out a second invoice, and levying penalties, such as extra fees at a certain deadline.

When it comes to the invoices that you have, you want to make sure that you have a plan in the event one of your customers doesn't pay their bill to you yet, since this can influence the cash flow so much. Come up with a plan of what you will need to do if the customer is thirty, sixty, or ninety days late on an invoice that you sent them.

Don't fall into the trap of thinking that once you sent out an invoice to a customer, that your bills are taken care of. Every late payment is basically an interest-free loan, and it is going to seriously harm the cash flow of your business. You want to keep sending out invoices and have a good plan in place to ensure that you are getting the message out to your customer and that they will pay for the product or service.

Chapter 30. Bookeeping Tips For Large Scale Business

Large cooperation different from the small scale business and require professional accountants to manage their books. The owners cannot take the risk of keeping records of the day to day transactions of businesses and have to be handled by professionals.

What do we mean by large scale business or cooperation?

A large scale business encompasses huge transactions, business deals and coverage rather than a small scale business. They have lots of workers and departments that keep the business running. It is difficult to actually place a minimum to classify a large scale business, but in terms of size and the amount of deals they pull, it is way larger than a small scale business.

The operation of big corporation usually exceeds their locality and their products or services travel long distance to their clients. The way in which the bookkeeping of corporations is handled is way different from that of the small business. Professional accountants will be needed to keep track of all operations in the organization and to maintain accurate books, payroll and taxes information.

In some cases, the company will outsource its accounting department to an accounting firm that will handle all the bookkeeping and account details of the company. The work involved here can be massive and can require a team of accountants lead by a team leader.

They will be sure to provide a financial statement to the owners or board of directors that oversees the care and running of the business. There are some similar things you will find with bookkeeping for a small scale businesses that you will also find in large scale corporations.

Here are some tips that are required for the running of the books in big company:

Getting a Team of Professional Accountants

There is no point in leaving the bookkeeping jobs for the owners to run. In such cases, professional accountants are required. The operation of a big corporation is much more complex than can be handled by small business. The professionals are well trained to handle situations that will occur in such large bases of operation. They are great at applying the best methods of bookkeeping available - the Accrual method and double bookkeeping method.

You do not necessarily have to go out looking for accountants to manage your books as you can outsource the job to an accounting firm. The accounting firm will take over the accounting department and ensure that your books are always kept up to date.

Accounting is very important in a business and you need the right firm with a good track record to ensure you get error free and efficient accounting. Some businesses have folded up because of improper accounting, which was caused by the inability of the accounting department to accurately manage a business.

In searching for an accounting firm, you should consider the following:

Ask around for credible accounting firms who deal within the same industry.

Search the history of the company to ensure that they do not have a bad record or criminal history.

Check for previous clients and the reviews they have given about the organization. If the firm is good at what they do, they will be happy to share references.

When you are working with a group of accountants, ensure not to mingle in their business. Give them room to operate and do their work at all times.

Always Check on the Accountant

You are running a big corporation and as the partner of your corporation and business affairs, it is important to get regular updates by checking on what they are doing. Ask for reports and demand that they provide financial statements at timely intervals.

Also, supervising the accountants will keep them on their toes to meet up with the deadline. If you leave them unsupervised or without deadline for tasks, they may lack the urgency and care for the work that you need them to do. One way to check on your accountant is to run an audit on the department with another accounting firm to ensure that they are not working against the best interests of the company.

Auditing is essential in big business and it is best done when you do not inform the accountants that it is going to be carried out. In all you do, you cannot cross check the work of your accountants by yourself, so you have to spend money to get your accountants checked out. Auditing is an important aspect of large business bookkeeping and accounting and goes beyond the scope of this book. Just keep it in mind as your business grows.

Open Accounts for all Forms of Transactions

When it comes to big business, you have a business account for your business with more than one signatory to the account. In running the day to day business, the accountant will be responsible for dealing with the accounting so they will be working along with the accounts department. If possible, the accountant will be part of the signatory to the account so they will be aware of the movement of funds and will be able to keep track of the transactions that occur in the business accounts.

If, on the occasion, the businesses have branches, then the area head accountant will have to submit financial statements from their sectors, which will be reconciled and one financial statement to be produced for the final financial statement of the business.

So, in this instance, all the individual branches must work together in reconciling accounts for the business to get the actual financial status of the business. There is an accounting team in the headquarters, usually that all the branches report to, and they end up making the final financial statement for the company. So the process of bookkeeping and accounting is a very complex process that requires much time and that is why it is important that the branches keep an accurate account so it will be easy to merge them and provide accurate results.

Make Use of Accounting Software

When you are dealing with the account of a big corporation, you will be dealing with huge loads of work. Most times doing this manually will not be possible, filled with errors and time consuming. Some accounting firms have their programmers that help them develop software that is suited for a particular company to meet their needs.

This software will help accountants to manage their bookkeeping, present financial statements, presentation and calculation of data. Many have training videos and written tutorials available on the platform that will show you how to use them or your firm can provide an in house tutorials for you. It is important to get your team working on the latest software available so they will be efficient in their work.

Companies should also allow their accountants to go for refresher courses that will show them ways to use the latest accounting software and methods.

Request Quarterly and Financial Statements

As the owners of the business, the best way to check on your business is to require quarterly statements and end of year financial statements. The financial decision of the business will be based on these statements that are given to the business owners to analyze and digest.

Also by making this request, the business owners are ensuring that the accountants are on their toes working hard to ensure proper accounting of the business and timely presentation of the reports requested.

Ensure the Use of the Latest Accounting Software

You have to keep up to date with the latest technology to keep your accounting safe, easy and efficient. There are regular updates of the software you are using, which will improve their capabilities and keep them safe from the latest malware. Malware can be a security threat and may damage your files, so stay secure and keep your software updated at all times. Most offices are now connected to the Internet and security is paramount to keeping company data safe. Hackers can creep into your network, steal company information or cause havoc that will affect the business.

And don't forget to backup! Daily, automatic backups are the easiest. Whatever you decide, be sure you are always backing up your info, even if it's just to the Cloud.

Keep Track of your Liabilities

You should keep track of your liabilities to ensure that they do not impact negatively on your business. Liability is anything that takes money away from your business and can become harmful when they exceed the assets of the company, and can indicate that the business is heading toward bankruptcy. There is some liability that is necessary for the business, but as a company you should always check your liabilities and make sure they remain at a manageable level.

Chapter 31.   Why You Need The
Knowledge Of Accounting

Do you really need bookkeeping in order to have a business?

The above question has been debated for a long time as people tend to analyze the importance of acquiring this knowledge regardless of which kind of business you have. Small business owners often end up learning bookkeeping as they carry out their basic daily tasks.

However, you still need to expand your knowledge with the available online and offline courses that will sharpen their knowledge. It is understandable for small business owners to learn some level of basic bookkeeping and accounting, but what about those who employ people to do these bookkeeping and accounting jobs for them?

Know How To Run Your Business

For the person that runs a personal business, knowledge of bookkeeping will help the person managing the business accounts. The basics may be needed to run a small-scale business, but one can go for advanced courses as the person seeks to know how to manage their business.

This book has provided you with the basic knowledge of bookkeeping and accounting and we have shown you how to make a simple accounting of your business. If you have accountants working for you then you'll be able provide them the proper documents needed for them to prepare and analyze your information, and in exchange, help to provide you accurate guidance.

It would be a mistake to leave yourself completely at the mercy of your accountant with no knowledge of your business's accounting rules. Do not make the mistake of being disinterested in bookkeeping and accounting, for this is where the money is calculated. It is your business and you are in charge, so you should know how the financial process of the business is going. Stay up to date with the bookkeeping as you check on the books and accounts of the company.

When the accountants are aware that you are knowledgeable about the accounts, they careful not to make mistakes and often enjoy working with a business owner that is knowledgeable and can talk "shop" with them. They will be less likely to attempt to cheat you, for they know you are aware of their activity in the business and how it works. When an accountant, bookkeeper or any financial advisor knows that you have no clue about your business, then you open yourself up to be taken advantage of.

Analyze Financial Reports

What will you do if your employee drops the monthly financial report on your desk? Do you have the knowledge to understand and know what it tells you about your business?

This is one of the important reasons for getting yourself equipped and learn to analyze the data. You can picture how your business is faring by looking at the data in front of you, which is important in making decisions.

What does your account sheet tell you when your expenses are higher than your income? You are experiencing losses as your sales and inventory does not tally, so what do you do?

In this first instant, when your expenses are more than what you make, obviously you have to cut down on what you are spending. Look out for what expenses can be reduced and in such cases that will not affect the outcome of the business. Such a decision will require some knowledge of accounting.

Now, in the second scenario, your books do not tally with what you make and your inventory. This is the time for you to take a look at the account sheets and find out what went wrong. It may be that you are experiencing a loss because your inventory is being tampered with, maybe by employee theft, for instance. They may be stealing from under your nose, since they know that you do not know how to take inventory. When you can take inventory, you can trace where this shortage in your inventory is coming from and then you may be able to trace exactly which employee is taking advantage of you. If your workers know you're on top of your business, they are less likely to steal.

Decision Making In The Boardroom

Your ability to make financial decision for your business, either in a personal business or in the boardroom, depends on your ability to make decisions based on what is placed in front of you. Take a look at the financial statements in front of you and make informed decisions rather than guess work. Even you are unsure, you will have enough knowledge to approach others for assistance and to collaborate.

Most board members are knowledgeable in reading financial reports and analyzing reports in order to make sound decisions. Remember, you don't have to be the novice at the table. You can learn and take control of your financial understanding.

Don't Get Cheated

Knowledge of accounting will be useful so you do not get cheated, either in your personal business or when making financial decisions. Imagine yourself as an investor who is seeking an opportunity to invest in a business. With the knowledge of bookkeeping and accounting, you can make favorable decisions. You will look at the report and be able to determine the health status of the business, as it will be a visible information rather than relying on what you are being told.

On the other hand, you are an important member of the company board and the accountant cooked up a phony statement. With your knowledge, you'll be able to scan through the papers and point out the red flags while you determine where the discrepancies are in the report.

As a business owner, you can determine your taxes and pay them on time and you can determine when a consultant is trying to play tricks on you.

Do not take the knowledge of accounting for granted in your business! Do not say that the aspect of accounting should be left solely in the hands of professional; get involved in your business. Your future depends on it.

Specialize In Specific Areas In Bookkeeping And Accounting

Now the world of bookkeeping and accounting is very broad and in your quest to learn, you might decide to specialize in some particular aspect. In the process, you might decide that you want to focus more on the investment part of accounting, or on bookkeeping or other areas and in the process become an expert in that field. There are people that are very good in the management of company data, in preparing taxes for companies, in reading financial reports and carrying out the necessary deductions using your own knowledge rather than relying upon others.

As you learn more about the accounting process, you may find a particular area you are interested in and decide to work in that area of specialization. You can become so knowledgeable that you are paid as a consultant to help others in that particular area of accounting.

As a board member, you might be interested in investment in other companies, so you take much effort to analyze the financial statements of companies to pick up the investment indices of the reports. You will work with those indices, such as income flow, balance sheets and sustainability of capital, as well as learning how well the company can make a profit. With these, you can easily analyze the business fortune of a company. As you become interested, take the time to study these indices as it becomes easier for you to pick up the right details as you can easily deduct the investment profitability of the company.

Others may be interested in other areas such as managing the expansion of a company, tax preparation of the company, inventory and other areas of bookkeeping and accounting.

Bookkeeping Increases Your Knowledge Of Business

As you learn bookkeeping, you become very knowledgeable in business structure because you are aware of every aspect of the business, be it the inventory, salary structure, money management etc., and this makes you a very important asset to your business and in business decision making. So, in essence, you can see that bookkeeping and accounting are no waste of time and everyone should at have a basic understanding of accounting. If you want to succeed to business, reduce spending and increase profit, you must know and understand you finances.

You Are In Command Of Your Business

With no knowledge of the simplest form of bookkeeping, you are left at the mercy of your accountant or employee (or friend or neighbor for that matter) to make your business decisions for you. When you are in this situation, you are left riding in the back putting others at the wheel, because you lack the ability to understand the basic decision making indices. You end up having to pay people to help you make decisions and you may not be aware of what is going on in the business. It is a set up for failure.

However, with basic knowledge of bookkeeping and accounting, you can partake in the decision making within your business. Because you know what you want for your business, you can make decisions that will suit you with the ability to read and understand the information from the financial sheets. In learning the basic knowledge of accounting, you may not be directly involved in the accounting process, but you will have the ability to read the information provided and be decisive.

Do not allow anybody to be the game changer in your business because you do not understand basic bookkeeping. Move into the driver's seat and take charge of your money, your decisions, your business and your life.

Conclusion

A closing process in accounting refers to the steps an accountant must take to review and zero out some accounts, like the income and expenses accounts, and then record the net profit or loss in the balance sheet. If you use accounting software to prepare your books, it will close your revenue and expense accounts automatically.

Most times, the closing process is always carried out by an accountant. However, a small business owner can use accounting software to accomplish this task. Your books need to be closed annually since you need to file income tax returns every year. It is a common practice among businesses to close their books monthly.

If you perform many transactions and your business is large, you might need to leave the closing process to your accountant. As a business owner, you should understand the process of closing the books, even if you are not doing it yourself. This will help you to know if your job was well done.

Closing your books for the year-end means that all your reports have been finalized. These reports reveal the financial performance of a business during an accounting period. Business owners are entitled to know the ups and downs of their business.

Closing entries are aspects of the accounting process that occur at the end of an accounting period. During the closing process, balances in temporary accounts are posted to permanent ones. These temporary accounts include dividends, income, and expense accounts.

There are different reasons you need to close your books. The main purpose of closing the books is to ensure that revenue generated and expenses incurred from a previous accounting year are not carried over to the current account year. The closing process also helps business owners have insight into the financial position of their business.

Small business owners should ensure that their books are closed at the end of the year to file income tax returns annually. When you close your books, you can easily detect any error in your bookkeeping and accounting system. Closing the books also help businesses prepare for the next accounting period.

When you close your books monthly, it makes it easier to carry out monthly tasks such as paying your suppliers, sending invoices to customers, reconciling bank statements, preparing the journal, and sending reports on sales tax to the state. The closing process also helps you create an outline and strategies for the next accounting period.